Fairies and Witches

Fairytales and Mysteries of the Supernatural

Fairies and Witches

Fairytales and Mysteries of the Supernatural

Karel Weinfurter

Translated by Kytka Hilmarová

CZECH REVIVAL
PUBLISHING

Fairies and Witches: Fairytales and Mysteries of the Supernatural.
Copyright © 2023 by Kytka Hilmarová

Czech Revival Publishing.
www.czechrevival.com
US+ 727-238-7884

The views expressed in this work are the author's own and may not reflect the opinions or policies of any organization or individual. The author's personal experiences and opinions are shared for entertainment and educational purposes. Readers are encouraged to form their own conclusions based on the content presented. The author assumes no responsibility for the reader's actions. References to people, organizations, or events are based on the author's translation, recollection, and/or interpretation. This work does not provide professional advice, and readers should consult experts in relevant fields for guidance.

Library of Congress Cataloging-in-Publication Data

Weinfurter, Karel 1867-1942
Hilmarova, Kytka 1964-
        Fairies and Witches: Fairytales and Mysteries of the Supernatural. / Kytka Hilmarová

Summary: "Fairies and Witches: Fairytales and Mysteries of the Supernatural" is a collection of enchanting and mysterious fairy tales that delve into the realms of magic, folklore, and the supernatural. Filled with captivating narratives, these tales transport readers to fantastical worlds where brave protagonists face daunting challenges, encounter mythical creatures, and navigate through extraordinary adventures. With elements of wonder, love, and the eternal battle between good and evil, this collection offers a glimpse into the timeless allure of fairy tales and the enduring fascination with the mystical and otherworldly.

ISBN-13: 978-1-943103-31-7

1. Literature & Fiction > Mythology & Folk Tales > Fairy Tales 2. Literature & Fiction > Mythology & Folk Tales > Folklore 3. Literature & Fiction > Short Stories & Anthologies > Short Stories

Immerse yourself in a world of enchantment and wonder with these captivating fairytales that will transport you to magical realms and ignite your imagination.

To those who live their lives full of wonder.

Table of Contents

Preface 1

The Devil and the Peasant 5

The Princess on the Fiery Mountain 15

The Enchanted Horse...........................29

Krakonoš..................................43

Strong Kubáň...........................49

Kašpárek and the Witch.......................67

The Blue Princess 83

Mister Dragon in the Yellow Mountain............111

The Magic Ring 131

Skřítek The Little Gnome 143

Little Tom Thumb...............................149

Werewolf 157

The Elf and the Cook 175

The Devil's Flute 189

Witches 201

The Shepherd and the Princess 207

About the Author 227

Translator's Note 237

About the Translator 239

Preface

Welcome to "Fairies and Witches: Fairytales and Mysteries of the Supernatural." In this enchanting collection, Karel Weinfurter shares a series of captivating fairytales that delve into the realms of fairies and witches, allowing readers to immerse themselves in the magical narratives created by this renowned Czech mystic.

As an English translation of these timeless tales, it is my great pleasure to present these stories to you. I sought to bring these enchanting fairytales from the original Czech to English, so that readers around the world can enjoy the wonders woven by the world-renowned Czech mystic, Karel Weinfurter.

Within the pages of "Fairies and Witches," you will find a collection of fairytales that have been cherished for generations. Through these stories, Weinfurter unravels the mysteries surrounding fairies and witches, exploring their significance in folklore, spirituality, and human imagination. While his focus is primarily on sharing the tales themselves, his profound understanding of the subject matter adds an extra layer of depth to each narrative.

As you embark on this journey through the mystical realms, be prepared to be transported to worlds where fairies dance under the moonlight and witches weave spells under the starry skies. These tales, meticulously crafted by Weinfurter, capture the essence of folklore, spirituality, and human imagination.

While the focus of this book is primarily on sharing the fairytales themselves, Weinfurter's profound understanding of the subject matter adds an extra layer of depth to each story. Through his vivid storytelling, he unravels the mysteries surrounding fairies and witches, allowing readers to explore their significance in folklore and their enduring place in the human imagination.

It is my hope that this English translation of "O vílách a čarodějích" originally published by in Prague by Alois Hynek in 1920, will ignite your imagination, inspire a sense of wonder, and allow English readers to connect with the enchantment that Weinfurter masterfully weaves within each story.

Enjoy your journey through the realms of fairies and witches and may the magic within these pages stay with you long after you have finished reading.

–*Kytka Hilmarová*

The Devil and the Peasant

Once upon a time, in a bygone era when devils still roamed the earth, there was a devil who found himself lost in a distant land. Unable to return to hell that day, he wandered aimlessly, growing increasingly famished without a clue of his whereabouts. Tormented by hunger, he desperately sought nourishment and stumbled upon a meager portion of food placed on a bench outside a humble cottage—a meager alms intended for beggars. Though well aware that he was forbidden from partaking in alms, his hunger gnawed at him so relentlessly that he succumbed to temptation and devoured the offering.

Soon after, a searing pain gripped his stomach, causing him to writhe in agony and unleash anguished screams. He was tortured for what seemed like an eternity, and when the pain finally subsided, he ascended into the air and hurtled back to hell headfirst. But upon his arrival at the gate, he was met with a disheartening sight—it stood closed, unyielding to his pleas. Finally, a voice echoed from behind the gate, belonging to another devil:

"Our master decrees that you shall not enter, for you have consumed alms meant for the destitute. As punishment, you must venture into the mortal realm and serve there for a span of seven years!"

"Thank you very much!" thought the devil, but he had no choice but to obey. So he returned to the earth and embarked on a quest to find employment. He roamed far and wide, yet everywhere he went, he faced rejection. The farmers had an abundance of workers, and in places where labor was scarce, no opportunities could be found. Eventually, news reached the devil of a peasant in need of a helping hand, so he approached him earnestly, beseeching to be taken into service.

"I have no need for a farmhand," the peasant replied. "I possess only two weary horses, spent from serving the lord, and I can barely manage them. My field is meager, providing just enough sustenance for our meager existence. How could I possibly support an additional burden such as yourself?"

"Master," implored the devil, "please consider accepting me! I will toil as if I were three men, and when the harvest thrives, there shall be plenty for all!" He persisted with his pleas until, finally, the peasant relented and agreed to take him on as a farmhand. Yet, deep down, the peasant harbored doubts, convinced that the young farmhand would soon flee due to hunger. The following day, the new farmhand approached the peasant in the living room and inquired, "Master, I have already tended to the horses. What tasks await us today?"

The peasant, having a small amount of grain in the field, informed the farmhand that they would proceed to harvest and thresh it without delay. They sat down for breakfast, and after satisfying their hunger, they made their way to the field. As the farmhand loaded the wagon, the peasant, observing the increasing weight, interjected, "That shall suffice, for the horses can bear no more!"

"Nay, they can manage," retorted the farmhand confidently, proceeding to load the remaining grain. Surprisingly, the horses pulled the burden as if it were weightless. Astonished, the peasant marveled at the strength displayed by his supposedly feeble steeds but refrained from commenting. Upon their return home, as the farmhand unharnessed the horses and led them to the stable, the peasant joined the other workers in the threshing field. Meanwhile, the farmhand climbed onto the wagon and commenced tossing the sheaves with such vigor that grains spilled out in every direction. The peasant, curious, approached and picked up a sheaf, finding it unusually light. Examination revealed not a single grain within. This discovery held true for each sheaf. All appeared to have been meticulously threshed. The peasant couldn't contain his astonishment, yet he refrained from questioning the farmhand.

In the following days, the farmhand's diligent work and attentive care transformed the horses into the finest in the entire region. The overall productivity of the farm flourished, and within a year, the peasant not only possessed outstanding equine companions but also acquired a substantial plot of land. The harvests were bountiful, and prosperity smiled upon him. He purchased two cows, renovated the cottage, and his newfound success did not go unnoticed by the neighboring farmers. They witnessed the remarkable turn of events since the arrival of the enigmatic farmhand and sought to entice him away to their own lands. Yet, the farmhand declined all offers, firmly committed to improving the life of the peasant. Whenever wages were mentioned, the farmhand dismissed the notion, proclaiming, "We shall settle it later. Time is aplenty!"

There existed but one peculiarity that troubled the peasant. On Sundays, when the community gathered for worship, the farmhand would also depart, yet never was he seen within the church. Perplexed, the peasant hesitated to question his companion, fearing offense might drive the farmhand away. Meanwhile, news of the peasant's newfound fortunes and his magnificent horses reached the ears of the castle's lord—a prince known for his cruelty and penchant for tormenting his subjects. One day, a servant arrived from the castle bearing an order for the peasant to appear before the prince the following morning. Obediently, the peasant arrived at the castle, cap in hand, and was ushered into the presence of the prince.

"I have heard of your fine horses and the strength of your farmhand," the prince declared. "To verify these claims, I hereby command you to transport a rock to the castle courtyard by tomorrow morning—the very rock that stands beneath the mill."

Startled, the peasant mustered his courage and implored, "Your Grace, I beseech you to reconsider. The rock is of immense size—no wagon can bear its weight, nor can any horses pull it!"

But the prince remained resolute. "You will carry out my command!" he retorted before dismissing the peasant.

Dejected, the peasant returned home, weighed down by the realization that the task assigned to him was insurmountable. As he arrived at his doorstep, he encountered the farmhand, who inquired, "What ails you, Peasant? Why do you wear such a crestfallen countenance?"

Reluctantly, the peasant shared the order he had received and bemoaned the misfortune that had befallen him. "Oh, dear lad, it seems impossible to fulfill the prince's demand," sighed the peasant, his spirits low.

Fear not," reassured the farmhand with a smile. "The rock shall arrive in the castle courtyard as the prince desires."

The peasant's eyes widened in disbelief. "Are you out of your mind?" he exclaimed. "Even if we gathered an army of people and harnessed the strongest horses, no wagon could withstand the weight!"

Unperturbed, the farmhand chuckled softly and replied, "Worry not, peasant. All shall be accomplished. Rest now, and you shall witness the fulfillment of the prince's command."

Though filled with doubt, the peasant couldn't resist the flicker of hope ignited by the farmhand's words. Throughout the night, his mind swirled with questions, yet something held him back from seeking answers.

At dawn, the farmhand rose early, tending to the horses with meticulous care. The peasant joined him, mounting one steed while the farmhand took the other. Together, they embarked on their journey to the castle. As they neared the bridge, the prince appeared at an open window, eagerly anticipating their arrival. Upon reaching the castle courtyard, they discovered a carriage already prepared. With swift efficiency, they harnessed the horses, and the prince entered the carriage. The farmhand positioned himself on the driver's seat, while the peasant settled on the back seat for the footmen. And so, their peculiar journey commenced.

The horses surged forward, their hooves barely touching the ground as they galloped with remarkable speed. Suddenly, a gust of wind swept off the peasant's hat, sending it flying behind them. Distressed, he cried out, "Wait, farmhand, my hat has been lost!"

But the farmhand merely glanced back and chuckled, "Peasant, your hat has already journeyed to the seventh kingdom. You shall find it upon your return."

Bewildered, the peasant marveled at the fleeting sense of time as they continued their rapid progress. After a while, they arrived at a wide river, spanning across it a magnificent black bridge. Crossing the bridge, they entered an expansive green plain, devoid of any trees, stretching as far as the eye could see. Halting their carriage on this verdant expanse, the prince promptly disembarked, and the farmhand swiftly joined him. Sensing the impending significance of the moment, the peasant maneuvered the carriage, preparing for their return journey. It was then that a large black bird materialized before him, stirring a recollection of the farmhand's instructions. With trepidation, the peasant turned his gaze backward, and terror washed over him. Whipping the horses into action, he followed the bird's lead, for behind them, a maelstrom of flames, billowing smoke, and trembling earth threatened to consume everything in its path.

As the journey unfolded, the bird guided their path, and the peasant glimpsed his lost hat lying on the road. Days turned into weeks, yet he remained grateful for his foresight in bringing sufficient provisions. Eventually, they returned to familiar lands, where the peasant shared his incredible adventure, leaving everyone in awe. However, the prince and the enigmatic farmhand were never seen again.

The Princess on the Fiery Mountain

Long ago, there ruled a powerful king in a distant land, but he had no children, which saddened him greatly. The queen, too, was unhappy that God had not blessed them with an heir. One day, while she was walking in the royal garden, praying to God to grant her wish, a beautiful golden bee started flying around her head.

The queen noticed it, and the bee suddenly landed on her shoulder, buzzing sweetly. Then it flew a short distance and returned to sit on the queen's shoulder again. The queen found it remarkable, so she followed the bee, which flew ahead of her. Soon, the golden bee led her to a thicket. When the queen parted the bushes, she found a beautiful baby boy lying on the moss. She realized that God had sent her this child, so she took him and brought him to the castle.

When the king saw the beautiful child, he was overjoyed and adopted him as his own, naming the boy Vítězmir. But on the very first night, the queen woke up to find three women standing by Vítězmir's crib: one dressed in black and the other two in white. The queen was terrified and unable to move because she recognized them as powerful fairies.

The black fairy said, "When the child turns one year old, I decree that he shall be stolen by an evil dwarf and taken to an inaccessible forest!"

Then the second fairy in white spoke, saying, "And I grant him fearlessness and the greatest strength of all the heroes in the world!"

Finally, the third fairy, also in white, spoke and said, "And I bestow upon him the gift that when he turns twenty, he shall win the most beautiful bride in the world!"

After saying this, all three fairies disappeared, and the room grew dark. The queen couldn't sleep for a long time, pondering over this event. When she woke up in the morning, she believed it was all just a dream.

And so, twelve months passed, and one day, while Vítězmir was lying in the royal garden, surrounded by maids and nurses in his golden cradle, a thick fog suddenly enveloped them, rendering the maids unable to see anything. When the fog dissipated, Prince Vítězmir had vanished with it. Despite the king's orders to search diligently, the prince could not be found. There was great sorrow in the royal castle; the king and queen mourned despairingly, and the entire court and staff were filled with sadness because everyone loved the beautiful Vítězmir, for there was no child more adorable under the sun.

Meanwhile, Prince Vítězmír was abducted by the evil dwarf and taken into a dense forest. He had to lie on moss, and the dwarf fed him with deer's milk, strawberries, blueberries, roots, and took care of him without causing him harm. Vítězmír grew bigger and stronger, and when he turned six, the dwarf brought an enormous bear into the cave, which he had caught in the forest. He held the bear by the ears and led it.

Vítězmír said, "Eat him! Eat him! Little bear!" He provoked the bear against the frightened foster parent. However, when the bear tried to run, Vítězmír caught it by the ears and pulled it back as if it were a kitten. Then he drove the bear out of the cave and mocked the frightened foster parent.

Since then, the dwarf was extremely afraid of Vítězmír, but he still desired revenge and pondered how to achieve it. He decided to send Vítězmír to various parts of the forest where he knew ferocious wildlife resided, hoping they would be his demise. However, Vítězmír remained undaunted and fearlessly defeated every predator he encountered. Time passed until the prince's twentieth year drew near. Vítězmír yearned for adventure, but he lacked one essential thing—a proper sword.

Commanding the dwarf, Vítězmír declared, "Forge me a proper and sharp sword. Fail, and I will strangle you!"

Knowing he had no choice, the dwarf summoned all his magical skills to craft a sword that met Vítězmír's expectations. After several days of relentless effort, he presented the sword to the prince.

"Good. I shall test it immediately to ascertain its worthiness," Vítězmír proclaimed. He swung the sword above his head and struck it against the anvil, but to his disappointment, the blade broke. Furious, he threw the broken pieces at the dwarf's feet. "Do you dare to give me such a feeble piece? Forge me another sword, and it must be superior. Otherwise, I will strangle you!"

With fear coursing through his veins, the dwarf set to work once more. He poured all his skill and magic into forging a sword that surpassed the previous one. Finally, he presented it to Vítězmír.

"Good. I shall test it to determine if it suits me," Vítězmír declared. He swung the sword with full force, but once again, the blade shattered into fragments.

"You dare to offer me such a flimsy piece once more!" Vítězmír exclaimed angrily. He seized the broken pieces and cast them at the dwarf's feet. "If you fail to forge me a better sword, I will strangle you!"

Trembling with fear, the dwarf stammered, "Vítězmír, Vítězmír, it is futile. I cannot forge a better sword. However, I can share with you a secret. Deep in the heart of the forest stands a thousand-year-old oak tree, in which the renowned sword of the king of all wizards is embedded up to its hilt. If you possess the strength to draw that sword, you will wield the best blade in the world."

"Lead me to that oak," Vítězmír commanded resolutely.

And so, they embarked on their journey, traversing treacherous ravines and rugged terrain, pushing through dense thickets until they reached the towering oak tree. In the ancient oak, the sword of the legendary wizard was firmly lodged. With his mighty right hand, Vítězmír grasped the handle and effortlessly pulled it from the tree, a testament to his immense strength.

Returning home, Vítězmír tested the sword, striking the anvil with a single blow, splitting it in two. Yet, the sword remained unscathed.

"Now, I possess the sword I desired!" Vítězmír exclaimed triumphantly. "Tomorrow, I shall venture into the world and accomplish heroic deeds!"

"Go forth, Vítězmír!" the dwarf replied. "And I shall offer you advice for your first grand quest, one that will earn you great renown."

"Speak, then, dwarf," said Vítězmír.

"If you travel along the river for two days, you shall come upon the underground lair of an enormous dragon that guards a vast treasure. Within lies a ring imbued with the power to grant invulnerability and a helmet that renders its wearer invisible. However, the only way to access the treasure is by slaying the fearsome dragon. With your newfound sword, you may have a chance, if you are not afraid!"

"Fear? What is that?" Vítězmír questioned, his brave spirit unwavering.

Little did Vítězmír know, the old wizard and the dwarf harbored malicious intentions, confident that the dragon would devour him the moment he neared its lair. Undeterred, the following day, Vítězmír set forth on his grand adventure. He walked along the river's edge, his heart brimming with cheerfulness, occasionally breaking into song or playing a lively tune on his forest horn for amusement.

Finally, after days of unwavering determination, he arrived at the lair of the underground dragon, marked by the remnants of past victims strewn about. The dragon slumbered within its den, oblivious to the approaching threat. Vítězmír settled himself near the lair and patiently waited.

As time passed, a magnificent bird descended and perched upon a nearby tree, filling the air with its melodious song. Enthralled by the bird's music, Vítězmír sought to imitate its enchanting melody. He fashioned a whistle from reeds but found it unsatisfactory, discarding it in frustration. Turning to his trusted horn, he played his favorite tune with a resounding blast.

The sound reverberated through the air, reaching the ears of the slumbering dragon below. Stirred from its rest, the mighty creature emerged, sniffing the air for the scent of a human presence. Gradually, it appeared, its fiery eyes filled with anger.

"I was merely seeking a drink, but it seems I have stumbled upon a delectable morsel!" the dragon growled, preparing to pounce upon Vítězmír.

However, with unparalleled swiftness and unwavering determination, Vítězmír approached the dragon, his sword gleaming in the sunlight. In one swift motion, he thrust his blade into the dragon's heart, causing the colossal beast to collapse in defeat. The dragon's blood splattered onto Vítězmír's hand, and in a moment of instinct, he licked the crimson liquid. A surge of understanding coursed through him, allowing him to comprehend the language of all creatures.

The bird, previously singing in the tree, now spoke in a human voice. "Vítězmír, Vítězmír, come with me. I shall guide you to the fiery mountain where a beautiful princess awaits. But first, descend into the dragon's lair and claim the ring and helmet!"

With the bird as his guide, Vítězmír ventured into the dark depths of the lair. The further he descended, the brighter the light grew, until he found himself surrounded by a radiant treasure accumulated by the dragon over time. Gold and jewels glimmered, but Vítězmír's focus remained unwavering. He eschewed the riches and sought out the simple steel helmet and the ring of invulnerability, placing the ring upon his finger.

Emerging into the daylight, Vítězmír stood before the bird, ready to embark on the final leg of his quest. "Lead the way to the fiery mountain where the beautiful princess resides," he declared.

And so, Vítězmír followed the bird's ethereal flight, traversing mountains and valleys for seven days and seven nights until a radiant glow in the distance signaled their arrival at the fiery mountain. The bird disappeared, leaving Vítězmír at the wearer invisible. However, the only way to access the treasure is by slaying the fearsome dragon. With your newfound sword, you may have a chance, if you are not afraid!"

"Fear? What is that?" Vítězmír questioned, his brave spirit unwavering.

Little did Vítězmír know, the old wizard and the dwarf harbored malicious intentions, confident that the dragon would devour him the moment he neared its lair. Undeterred, the following day, Vítězmír set forth on his grand adventure. He walked along the river's edge, his heart brimming with cheerfulness, occasionally breaking into song or playing a lively tune on his forest horn for amusement.

Finally, after days of unwavering determination, he arrived at the lair of the underground dragon, marked by the remnants of past victims strewn about. The dragon slumbered within its den, oblivious to the approaching threat. Vítězmír settled himself near the lair and patiently waited.

As time passed, a magnificent bird descended and perched upon a nearby tree, filling the air with its melodious song. Enthralled by the bird's music, Vítězmír sought to imitate its enchanting melody. He fashioned a whistle from reeds but found it unsatisfactory, discarding it in frustration. Turning to his trusted horn, he played his favorite tune with a resounding blast.

The sound reverberated through the air, reaching the ears of the slumbering dragon below. Stirred from its rest, the mighty creature emerged, sniffing the air for the scent of a human presence. Gradually, it appeared, its fiery eyes filled with anger.

"I was merely seeking a drink, but it seems I have stumbled upon a delectable morsel!" the dragon growled, preparing to pounce upon Vítězmír.

However, with unparalleled swiftness and unwavering determination, Vítězmír approached the dragon, his sword gleaming in the sunlight. In one swift motion, he thrust his blade into the dragon's heart, causing the colossal beast to collapse in defeat. The dragon's blood splattered onto Vítězmír's hand, and in a moment of instinct, he licked the crimson liquid. A surge of understanding coursed through him, allowing him to comprehend the language of all creatures.

The bird, previously singing in the tree, now spoke in a human voice. "Vítězmír, Vítězmír, come with me. I shall guide you to the fiery mountain where a beautiful princess awaits. But first, descend into the dragon's lair and claim the ring and helmet!"

With the bird as his guide, Vítězmír ventured into the dark depths of the lair. The further he descended, the brighter the light grew, until he found himself surrounded by a radiant treasure accumulated by the dragon over time. Gold and jewels glimmered, but Vítězmír's focus remained unwavering. He eschewed the riches and sought out the simple steel helmet and the ring of invulnerability, placing the ring upon his finger.

Emerging into the daylight, Vítězmír stood before the bird, ready to embark on the final leg of his quest. "Lead the way to the fiery mountain where the beautiful princess resides," he declared.

And so, Vítězmír followed the bird's ethereal flight, traversing mountains and valleys for seven days and seven nights until a radiant glow in the distance signaled their arrival at the fiery mountain. The bird disappeared, leaving Vítězmír at the return brought an era of prosperity and unity. The realm basked in the glory of their brave prince, who had conquered dragons, mastered enchanted mountains, and won the heart of a captivating princess. The kingdom flourished under Vítězmír's wise and just rule, and his name echoed throughout the land as a symbol of courage and resilience.

The Enchanted Horse

Once upon a time, there lived a father with three sons. The first two sons were clever and astute, while the youngest, known for his foolishness, could do little more than bake cakes in the ashes. News arrived from the king, who sought to wed his eldest daughter. The man who could leap upon a horse and reach the princess, perched in a small house atop a lofty scaffolding, would win her hand.

Excitement spread throughout the kingdom, drawing crowds to the king's castle, including the two intelligent brothers. The third brother, lacking in understanding due to his dim-witted nature, struggled to comprehend the significance of the event. Fate, however, intervened when a mischievous devil sneaked into their small field and stole some of their freshly harvested wheat. Concerned about further losses, the brothers decided to assign their foolish sibling to guard the field the following night.

As darkness blanketed the land, the third brother gathered sticks and created three circles in the field, silently planning his strategy. He murmured to himself, outlining his plan.

"He who possesses good intentions shall remain within the first circle. The second circle shall confine the wicked, and should it be a devil, it shall continue its mischievous journey in the third."

While standing guard, the dim-witted brother noticed a figure approaching in the distance, engulfed in an eerie blaze. The ground quivered beneath the weight of each thunderous step, revealing the devil's presence. The devil swept through the field, seizing half of the wheat and preparing to flee.

Driven by determination, the foolish brother sprang into action. He swiftly threw a hoop around the devil's neck, challenging him with a bold declaration.

"Tear that hoop apart if you dare!" he exclaimed.

The devil effortlessly tore the hoop apart, undeterred by the brother's feeble attempt. Unfazed, the brother persisted and threw a second hoop around the devil's neck, taunting him further.

"Try tearing this one apart as well!" he exclaimed.

Again, the devil made quick work of the hoop, tearing it apart without hesitation. Undeterred, the foolish brother seized the moment and threw a third hoop around the devil's neck, his voice laced with determination.

"Now, tear this one apart if you can!" he exclaimed.

To his surprise, the devil faltered. He struggled in vain to break free from the third hoop, admitting defeat.

"I... I can't," the devil confessed.

With a triumphant smile, the brother seized the devil and posed a question.

"What shall you offer me in return for your freedom?" he asked.

The devil, realizing his predicament, offered a tempting proposition.

"I shall bestow upon you an enchanted horse. Enter through its left ear and exit through its right, and you shall transform into the most handsome man in the world," the devil promised.

Intrigued by the offer, the foolish brother eagerly inquired about the horse's whereabouts.

"Where may I find this magnificent horse of yours?" he asked.

With a whistle, the devil summoned the horse. It appeared before the brother, a magnificent creature with flames dancing in its nostrils, soaring three fathoms into the air.

"What shall you command, my master?" the horse inquired.

Without any specific instructions, the brother decided to put the horse to the test.

"Nothing of particular importance. I simply wished to assess your abilities," he remarked.

In a moment of curiosity and courage, the brother entered through the horse's left ear and emerged through its right. To his astonishment, his appearance underwent a remarkable transformation. Once plain and unremarkable, he emerged as the epitome of handsomeness, his features captivating and his presence commanding. The brother, now radiating with newfound confidence, bid farewell to the devil and released the enchanted horse.

With a heart brimming with joy, the transformed brother made his way back home. Climbing onto the oven where he once baked cakes, he couldn't contain his excitement.

Meanwhile, his two clever brothers embarked on a journey to see the princess. Upon their return, the transformed brother eagerly inquired about their experience.

"Tell me, is it as beautiful as they say? Oh, how I long to witness it myself!" he exclaimed.

His brothers, unable to recognize their once foolish sibling, laughed heartily and dismissed his words, deeming him unfit to partake in such grandeur. Undeterred, the transformed brother responded with a determined proclamation.

"Remember this, if you choose to leave me behind, you shall not forget me," he warned.

As the night gave way to a new day, the transformed brother awoke with a purpose. He ventured into the forest, carrying a small basket with him. Concealing the basket beneath a bush, he let out three resounding whistles, his voice filled with anticipation.

"Lively horse, Foolish Joseph calls upon you!"

In an instant, the devil's horse came charging towards him. The transformed brother entered through the horse's left ear and emerged through its right, his physical allure reaching unparalleled heights. With grace and elegance, he mounted the horse and commanded it to take him to the scaffolding where the princess resided in her small house.

In a flurry of galloping hooves, they swiftly arrived at the grand scene. The transformed brother witnessed the princess, guarded by the king's loyal army, while a multitude of hopeful suitors, including princes and knights, attempted to leap on horseback and ascend to the princess's abode. Yet, none succeeded in reaching her.

Observing the spectacle, the transformed brother issued a command to his horse.

"Leap halfway up the scaffolding, but no further," he instructed.

However, the devil's horse, brimming with determination, surged forward, effortlessly surpassing the entire scaffolding. Gasps of astonishment filled the air as onlookers questioned whether it was a mere mortal or something otherworldly. The feat of the horse's boundless leap left everyone awestruck.

Unfazed by the commotion, the transformed brother swiftly rode back home on his horse. Along the way, he crossed paths with his brothers, who were returning from their unsuccessful pursuit of the princess. Sensing their presence, he discreetly acknowledged their presence, ensuring they remained unaware of his true identity. With a swift movement of his riding crop, he struck each brother on their back, leaving them astonished and bent in surprise.

Returning to the forest, the transformed brother bid farewell to his faithful horse, releasing it to freedom. As the horse galloped away, his outward appearance reverted to its former state of plainness and foolishness. Back in his parents' house, he resumed his place on the oven, continuing his familiar task of baking cakes.

While his brothers slumbered through the night, they set out once more to see the king's daughter the next morning. Observing their departure, the transformed brother pleaded with them to include him in their journey. However, his brothers scoffed at his request, belittling his intellect and deeming him unworthy of their company.

"Wait and see, for you shall remember me!" the transformed brother exclaimed as his brothers departed.

Undeterred by their rejection, he retraced his steps into the forest, carrying his trusted basket. Instead of collecting mushrooms as he had done before, he let out three resounding whistles and summoned his loyal horse. The transformation took place once again as he entered through the horse's left ear and emerged as the embodiment of irresistible charm and beauty.

Mounted on his majestic steed, the transformed brother rode through the astonished crowds, their eyes unable to look away from his captivating presence. With unwavering determination, he commanded the horse to leap as high as it could, aiming to reach out to the princess. The horse, fueled by both power and grace, soared through the air, defying gravity and surpassing all expectations. In a breathtaking display, the transformed brother extended his hand towards the princess, leaving the spectators in awe of his audacity.

Though only a fleeting moment, it left an indelible mark on the princess. She adorned him with a radiant symbol on his forehead and presented him with a golden ring bearing her name. Filled with gratitude and admiration, the transformed brother bid farewell to the princess, his heart brimming with joy.

With a final leap, he dismounted from the horse and released it, allowing it to gallop back into the realm of legends. As the horse vanished from sight, the external façade of beauty faded, leaving the transformed brother to revert to his former appearance.

Returning home, he carefully concealed the golden ring by coating it with tar, ensuring its brilliance remained hidden. He also wrapped a scarf around his head, concealing the symbolic mark bestowed upon him by the princess. When his father noticed these peculiarities, he inquired about the scarf.

"Why do you tie that scarf around your head?" his father asked.

"It's merely to alleviate a terrible headache," the transformed brother replied with a wry smile.

News of the princess's quest to find her betrothed spread like wildfire. The king, determined to identify the one who had leaped to his daughter's abode, summoned his subjects to assemble. The men stood in rows, while the princess embarked on a diligent search, hoping to recognize her beloved among them.

Days turned into nights, but the princess's quest remained unfulfilled. Frustration loomed in the air, prompting the king to make a desperate proclamation.

"Is there anyone among my subjects still absent?" the king exclaimed, pulling up his vest in a theatrical gesture.

The transformed brother's brothers, remembering their foolish sibling, spoke up without hesitation.

"We still have a brother at home, considered the most foolish of all," they proclaimed.

Despite their objections, the king dispatched his coachman with a splendid carriage, pulled by six magnificent horses, to bring the transformed brother to the royal palace. However, defying the king's expectations, the transformed brother chose to remain at home, deferring the invitation. The king, not one to give up easily, dispatched the carriage once more, this time with even greater grandeur. But again, the transformed brother declined the offer, and the carriage returned empty-handed.

Determined to bring the transformed brother to the palace, the king's brother took matters into his own hands. Witnessing the peculiar sight of an oven rolling out of the transformed brother's home and into the palace courtyard, an old soldier grabbed hold of the transformed brother's coat. In the chaos that ensued, the transformed brother managed to slip away, evading capture. The oven, a silent witness to it all, reached a vast field where the transformed brother let out three resounding whistles.

The familiar sound summoned his faithful horse, running swiftly towards him. Once again, the transformed brother entered through the horse's left ear and emerged radiating with regal charm and grace. Bathed in an aura of brilliance, he rode towards the palace, captivating all who witnessed his grand entrance.

With a daring leap, the transformed brother and his horse burst through the first-floor window, landing gracefully in the grand hall where the entire royal family was feasting. The room fell into a hushed silence as everyone recognized the transformed brother, their astonishment mixed with admiration. The king himself, overcome with joy, welcomed him with open arms and granted him a place of honor beside the princess.

A joyous wedding followed, uniting the transformed brother and the princess in holy matrimony. The kingdom celebrated their union, rejoicing in the tale of the humble and foolish brother who had emerged as a symbol of courage, resilience, and unexpected beauty. The transformed brother's newfound wisdom and charm shone brightly, endearing him to all.

From that day forward, the transformed brother and the princess lived a life filled with love, prosperity, and happiness. Their reign brought prosperity to the kingdom, as they governed with compassion and wisdom. The transformed brother's two clever brothers, who had once mocked him, now stood by his side as loyal companions, realizing the true worth hidden beneath his former foolishness.

And so, the tale of the transformed brother, from his humble beginnings as Foolish Joseph to his rise as a remarkable and beloved figure, spread far and wide. It became a legend whispered by parents to their children, inspiring them to look beyond appearances and value the depth of character within.

And they all lived happily ever after.

Krakonoš

In a remote village near Poniklá, there resided a destitute family that had endured a series of misfortunes. Despite their hardships, they clung to the hope that divine intervention would eventually grace their lives. The family, consisting of a man, a woman, and their three children, faced the additional burden of an epidemic that befell them. All three children fell ill, and in due course, the father succumbed to the same affliction, rendering him unable to work. When conventional remedies and homemade potions proved futile, the weary mother set out one day to the neighboring village in search of the renowned herbalist, Vlasáková. It was widely believed that she possessed profound knowledge of herbs, capable of healing a wide array of maladies, not just physical injuries, but almost any ailment. The woman's heart brimmed with hope, as she sought Vlasáková's aid for her ailing children and husband. She carried with her a small token, a piece of cloth, to express her gratitude should the herbalist provide assistance. Through the dense forest she ventured toward the hill where Vlasáková dwelled.

Suddenly, a grey-haired hunter, accompanied by his faithful canine companion, emerged from the thicket. Observing the woman's tearful countenance, he halted and inquired, "Why do you weep so profusely? Your eyes bear the reddened marks of sorrow."

The woman proceeded to explain the dire circumstances surrounding her family – the three sickly children and her ailing husband. She recounted their extreme poverty, where people turned a blind eye, refusing to aid them without financial recompense.

"And where are you headed?" asked the hunter.

"I am on my way to see old Vlasáková," the woman replied with hopeful anticipation. "I pray she will provide me with herbs or offer guidance on how to proceed."

"Do you truly believe that Vlasáková can offer you assistance?" the inquisitive hunter pressed on.

"Why should I not harbor such hopes?" the woman responded. "After all, she has successfully healed countless individuals, even when doctors were left helpless."

"Well then, let us discover who can aid you first!" declared the hunter, offering a suggestion. "Take hold of this leash and keep my dog by your side momentarily. I shall venture into the nearby forest to gather herbs."

The woman grasped the leash, assuming responsibility for the hunter's loyal canine companion, while he disappeared into the verdant depths. To her surprise, he swiftly reappeared, presenting her with three delicate blue flowers.

"Take these," he instructed, "brew them and administer the decoction to your husband and children. Witness the relief it shall bestow upon them!"

Meanwhile, during the hunter's absence, his devoted canine companion became entangled in a thorny bush by the roadside, sustaining painful scratches. Sensing the dog's predicament, the hunter gathered the thorny branches, placing them within the woman's apron.

"Offer this thorny bush to your goat," he advised, "for it shall bring you abundant blessings!"

The woman, perplexed by the unexpected gift of thorny branches, gazed up to express her gratitude, only to find the hunter and his dog had vanished. Overwhelmed with anticipation, she hastened home, eager to prepare the healing concoction for her suffering family.

Upon entering the humble abode, she first attended to the goat, casting the thorny branches before it. Then, she kindled the fire and brewed the blue flowers, creating a potent remedy for her ailing loved ones. The father and children consumed the concoction, and as if touched by a magical spell, they descended into a deep slumber.

"Perhaps these herbs hold the key to their recovery," whispered the woman, a glimmer of hope dancing in her eyes. She hurriedly made her way to the stable, where the goat awaited her attention.

To her astonishment, she discovered a gleam amidst the straw. Her hand reached out, grasping the object, feeling its coolness and weight. When she held it up to the light, she gasped in awe, realizing she held a substantial piece of pure gold. She crossed herself, her mind racing, as she noticed yet another pile of gold hidden amidst the straw, and then another, and another. Overwhelmed with joy, she wished to burst into the living room and share the incredible turn of events with her husband and children. It was now evident to her that she had encountered Krakonoš[1], the legendary mountain spirit. However, a sense of caution prevailed, as she remembered that her family still slumbered and must not be

---

[1] The term "Krakonoš" refers to a legendary figure known as "Krakonoš the Mountain Spirit" or "Krakonoš the Giant" in English. Krakonoš is a mythical character associated with the Krkonoše Mountains, a mountain range in the Czech Republic and Poland. In folklore, Krakonoš is portrayed as a powerful and benevolent spirit who punishes the wicked and rewards the good. He is often depicted as an old man with a long beard and a staff, and he plays a significant role in local legends and tales.

disturbed. She discreetly concealed the treasure within a chest, ensuring its safekeeping, and proceeded to milk the goat.

To her amazement, the goat produced an extraordinary quantity of milk, surpassing anything she had witnessed before. It seemed as though the bountiful flow mirrored the newfound blessings bestowed upon her family.

Before long, the father awoke, followed by the children, and they felt invigorated, as if a heavy burden had been lifted. Fortune smiled upon the entire household, and the mother eagerly revealed the tale of the goat's miraculous milk and the golden blessings. From that moment onward, the goat's milk never ceased to flow, and the family, once steeped in poverty, flourished as the happiest in the entire region. Each day, they offered fervent gratitude to God for the intervention of Krakonoš, whose benevolence had lifted them from the depths of despair.

Strong Kubáň

Once upon a time, there lived a blacksmith who had two sons. These extraordinary boys possessed such incredible strength that by the tender age of five, they were already grown men. There was no one in the world who could match their power. Eager to pass down his craft, their father invited them to join him in the forge and learn the art of ironworking.

Placing a piece of iron on the anvil, the blacksmith instructed his sons to strike it with their hammers. The older son, named Kubáň, swung his hammer with such force that the iron shattered into pieces and even caused the anvil's support to sink into the ground. Filled with fear, their father exclaimed, "I cannot work with you! Your strength would ruin every task!" He then turned to the younger son and asked him to strike the iron. Although the iron shattered once again, the anvil stood firm.

"You shall be my apprentice," the father declared, "but remember to wield a lighter hammer and exercise gentleness." The younger son agreed, content to stay and learn from his father. However, Kubáň, eager to gain experience, set off into the world. His father provided him with some money and guidance on which path to take.

Venturing into a vast forest, Kubáň encountered a mysterious old man. This hermit possessed prophetic abilities and an air of mystique. Halting Kubáň's journey, the hermit inquired about his destination. When Kubáň shared his intention of seeking experience in the world, the old man advised, "Proceed a little further in this direction, and you will come across a large stone on your right. Move it aside, and beneath it, you will discover a cave housing a golden horse. Take it with you."

As quickly as the hermit appeared, he vanished, leaving Kubáň to follow his instructions. True to the hermit's words, Kubáň located the stone, revealing the hidden cave and the magnificent golden horse within. Mounting the horse, he resumed his journey. After a considerable time, he reached a crossroad where two countries intersected. Standing proudly at the border was a pillar adorned with signposts indicating the directions. One signpost read, "The path to the land of the weak," while the other proclaimed, "The path to the land of the strong."

Deep in thought, Kubáň contemplated his choices before decisively opting for the path to the land of the strong. Riding on for hundreds of miles, he encountered neither villages nor houses—only an endless expanse of barren plain devoid of life. As day turned into night, hunger gnawed at him. However, after covering fifty more miles, he finally stumbled upon a small cottage.

Entering the humble dwelling, Kubáň discovered two elderly couples who seemed to be living in abject poverty. He humbly requested some food, but the aged residents sorrowfully replied, "What can we offer you? We possess nothing ourselves!" Nonetheless, they offered him a meager piece of bread.

Resuming his journey, Kubáň soon encountered a bear blocking the road. Reflexively reaching for his crossbow, he aimed at the bear, ready to strike. To his astonishment, the bear spoke with a human voice, pleading, "Do not shoot! I may prove useful to you someday!" Moved by the bear's words, Kubáň refrained from releasing the arrow, and the bear swiftly bounded after his horse.

Further along, he came across a dog and, once again, readied his crossbow. Yet, the dog spoke, appealing, "Do not shoot! I may prove useful to you someday!" Kubáň, recognizing the pattern, withheld his arrow, and the dog joined the bear in trailing alongside his horse.

Finally, a fox appeared before him in the forest. Kubáň, feeling a sense of déjà vu, hesitated to raise his crossbow. The fox, with a pleading gaze, implored, "Do not shoot! I may prove useful to you someday!" Respecting the words of the wise hermit and the peculiar animals he had encountered, Kubáň refrained from harming the fox. True to its word, the fox joined the bear and the dog, forming a unique entourage accompanying Kubáň on his journey.

Continuing his path, Kubáň eventually reached a bustling town. He halted in front of an inn, where he entrusted the innkeeper with the care of his horse, bear, dog, and fox, instructing him to secure them in the stable. Then, stepping into the tavern, he ordered a glass of wine, savoring its taste as he gazed out of the window onto the bustling street.

Among the throngs of people rushing towards the sea coast, Kubáň observed a scene of distress, with almost everyone in tears. Curiosity piqued, he inquired of the innkeeper, "Why are these people running towards the sea? And why is sorrow etched on every face?"

The innkeeper sighed, his voice tinged with sadness, as he replied, "They are escorting the princess to the shore, for the devil is coming to claim her!"

Perplexed, Kubáň sought further understanding, asking, "But why is the princess being handed over to the devil?"

With empathy and patience, the innkeeper unfolded the tale. "Some time ago, the king was sailing at sea when his ship struck a treacherous rock, leaving all aboard seemingly lost. But just as despair settled in, the devil emerged from the depths and offered the king a deal. He said, 'If you give me something you don't know about, I will free you.'"

Eager to secure his freedom, the king, convinced of his knowledge about his kingdom and family, accepted the devil's proposition. The innkeeper continued, "Little did the king know that during his absence, a daughter was born, unbeknownst to him. Thus, he unwittingly promised the devil his own child."

Absorbing this revelation, Kubáň determinedly expressed his desire, "May I go and see the princess?"

The innkeeper, recognizing the resolute determination in Kubáň's eyes, nodded and granted his request. Kubáň issued one final instruction, "If I do not return, open the stable and release my animals."

With resolve fueling his steps, Kubáň embarked on his journey towards the sea. Despite the late hour, he forged ahead, the fervor in his heart outshining the fading daylight. As he approached the shore, the commotion subsided, and the crowd dispersed, leaving only the princess confined within a barrel.

Unbeknownst to them, a young knight, deeply enamored with the princess, perched atop a crown of an oak tree, hoping to witness the devil's arrival. Kubáň spotted the knight's presence but chose not to reveal himself. Instead, he quietly approached the barrel, climbing inside and remaining hidden alongside the princess. As midnight approached, nature itself seemed to hold its breath, a foreboding stillness enveloping the surroundings. Suddenly, a black cloud emerged from the sea, the earth trembled, and the sky crackled with the fury of a storm. Amidst this tumultuous display, the devil materialized before the barrel, his presence commanding attention. With a voice tinged with menace, the devil addressed the hidden occupants, demanding, "How many are inside? Should I tear you both apart, or just one of you?"

Fearless and quick-witted, Kubáň replied, his words laced with defiance, "It would be better for you to bite into an onion and taste its flavor!"

Enraged by Kubáň's audacity, the devil's eyes blazed with fury. "You may be clever with your words," he seethed, "but let us see if you possess the strength to match!"

Meanwhile, back at the inn, a tremendous commotion erupted within the stable as Kubáň's horse, driven by an innate sense of loyalty, yearned to break free. Unbeknownst to the forgetful innkeeper, the bear, dog, and fox joined the horse in their determination. Together, their combined might proved unstoppable, as they shattered the stable doors and thundered toward the sea.

Seizing the opportunity, Kubáň proposed to the devil, "Before we engage in combat, let our horses face each other in battle."

Agreeing to this unconventional suggestion, the devil unleashed his steed, and Kubáň handed the princess a knife, instructing her, "If my horse's reins become entangled, cut them without hesitation."

With a thunderous clash, the horses clashed in a fierce struggle. In the end, Kubáň's golden horse proved superior, overpowering and tearing apart the devil's horse. Emboldened by this victory, Kubáň turned to the devil, his gaze unwavering. "Now," he declared, "it is time for us to confront each other."

The devil, no longer underestimating Kubáň's strength, approached him, his voice dripping with malice. "Shall we fight ourselves or let our horses decide our fate?"

Kubáň, undeterred, responded, "Let our horses rest. This battle is ours to settle."

With their horses aside, Kubáň and the devil faced each other, the weight of their confrontation palpable. "Strike me across the ears," Kubáň challenged.

The devil obliged, striking Kubáň with a force that caused him to sink into the ground, the earth enveloping his ankles. Yet, Kubáň stood firm, his determination unyielding. In turn, Kubáň delivered a blow that sent the devil sinking, his form disappearing into the earth until only his head remained exposed. Unrelenting, Kubáň struck the devil once more, severing his head from his body.

With the devil defeated, Kubáň placed a colossal boulder upon his lifeless form, ensuring his demise. Then, turning to the princess, he offered his hand and said, "Come, let us return to your kingdom. Be my wife but swear to me that your heart will never belong to another."

The princess, filled with gratitude and admiration for Kubáň's bravery, pledged her loyalty. Together, they embarked on the journey back to the castle, where the king awaited their arrival.

However, the young knight, fueled by jealousy and desperation, caught up to the princess and confronted her, demanding her hand in marriage. But the princess, wise and resolute, rejected his advances. "How can I be your wife?" she retorted. "You did not save me from the devil's clutches!"

Enraged by her rejection, the knight threatened her, uttering vile words. Yet, the princess, fortified by her recent ordeal and her faith in a higher power, remained steadfast.

Unperturbed by the knight's threats, the princess pressed forward, determined to reach the castle. With each step, her resolve grew stronger, for she knew that if she had been saved from the clutches of the devil, she would also be protected from the hands of this unworthy suitor.

Arriving at the castle, the princess approached her father, the king, and made a heartfelt plea, "Father, I beseech you, grant me half an hour to contemplate my fate."

The king, touched by his daughter's plea, granted her request, eager to see her happiness restored. In her chamber, the princess hastily penned a letter to her true savior, Kubáň, urgently calling him to her side. She poured her heart into every word, expressing her undying gratitude and love.

Unbeknownst to the princess, the king happened upon the letter, his eyes scanning the heartfelt message. Realizing the truth behind his daughter's affections, he carefully folded the letter, keeping its contents to himself.

In a swift motion, the king summoned an officer and issued a command, "Go to the inn with a contingent of soldiers and bring me the man who seeks to marry my daughter."

The officer, dutiful and resolute, arrived at the inn and confronted the innkeeper, his voice hushed. "Where is the man who seeks to marry the king's daughter?"

The innkeeper, aware of Kubáň's immense strength, urged caution, whispering, "Speak softly, for he is a man of extraordinary power who could easily overpower you."

However, the officer remained undeterred. "I have a squad of soldiers at my disposal," he replied, his confidence unshaken. But as fate would have it, Kubáň emerged from his room, overhearing their conversation. With a knowing smile, he confronted the officer, questioning the disturbance.

Blinded by his own arrogance, the officer jeered at Kubáň, unaware of the strength that lay within him. In an instant, Kubáň seized the officer by his leg, effortlessly carrying him out of the inn, and swiftly incapacitated the accompanying soldiers, save for one. Turning to the lone survivor, he commanded, "Return to the king and inform him to gather twenty strong soldiers to come and fetch me."

Not long after, a colonel arrived at the inn, accompanied by twenty soldiers. Sensing the gravity of the situation, the colonel approached the innkeeper cautiously, seeking information. The innkeeper, having witnessed Kubáň's might, urged the colonel to exercise caution. However, the colonel, too, carried an air of unwavering confidence, believing that his forces could overcome any obstacle.

As Kubáň emerged once more, the colonel addressed him, his voice tinged with authority. Kubáň's eyes narrowed, taking in the scene before him. "Why do you cause such a commotion, shouting so loudly?" he inquired.

In a display of his prodigious strength, Kubáň seized the colonel by his legs, leading him outside where he dispatched the entire squad of soldiers. Only one remained, trembling in fear. Kubáň spoke sternly, "Go to the king and deliver this message: Gather all the people of your kingdom, as well as those from other realms, and bring forth the largest cannon you possess."

Word of Kubáň's command reached the king, filling him with equal parts trepidation and curiosity. Accompanied by a vast army and the entire population, the king arrived at the inn, bearing the largest cannon in his arsenal, drawn by twelve mighty horses. The sight that unfolded before their eyes left them awestruck and speechless.

Kubáň, standing tall and resolute, looked upon the gathered crowd and addressed the king, his voice carrying an air of authority. "Have you brought everything as I commanded?"

The king, his voice quivering, replied, "Yes, everything is here, as you requested."

Kubáň's eyes fell upon the colossal cannon, harnessed to the twelve horses. A smile played at the corners of his lips as he reached out, effortlessly lifting the massive weapon with a strength that defied belief. With surprising ease, he filled the cannon with tobacco and lit it, the smoke swirling around him as he held it like a pipe.

The onlookers gasped in disbelief; their eyes fixed on the inconceivable sight before them. The king, overcome with fear, fell to his knees, his voice trembling as he uttered, "I am not worthy to stand before you, mighty Kubáň. It is I who should kneel before you."

Kubáň, his demeanor gentle and magnanimous, placed his hands on the king's shoulders and lifted him back to his feet. "Rise, Your Majesty," he said with humility. "We shall stand as equals, for your daughter's happiness is my greatest desire."

Turning to the gathered crowd, Kubáň commanded, "Where is the man who took the princess from the seashore? Show us where he hid the devil and his severed head."

The young knight, pale with guilt and trepidation, stepped forward, his voice faltering. "The devil is hidden by the shore, beneath a large stone," he confessed. "And his severed head hangs in the crown of a nearby tree."

Kubáň, along with the king and the knight, made their way to the shore. Standing before the great stone, Kubáň commanded the knight, "Roll away the stone and reveal the devil's resting place."

But the knight hesitated, fear paralyzing him. Sensing the knight's lack of resolve, Kubáň, with a single powerful kick, sent the stone flying, exposing the pit where the devil lay.

The king leaned over, peering into the depths, while the knight cowered in fear.

Approaching the trembling knight, Kubáň laid a hand on his shoulder. "Now you see the truth, my king," he spoke softly but firmly. "It was not this knight who saved your daughter, but it was I who fought the devil and triumphed."

The king, his eyes filled with regret, turned to Kubáň, his voice heavy with remorse. "You have proven yourself to be the true savior of my daughter, Kubáň. I offer you my deepest apologies for my blindness."

Kubáň, ever gracious, accepted the king's apology with a nod. The people, witnessing this display of strength and humility, erupted in cheers and applause, their admiration for Kubáň resounding through the air.

And so, Kubáň was hailed as a hero, and the kingdom rejoiced. A grand celebration was held, and amidst the revelry, Kubáň and the princess were united in marriage, their love and courage celebrated by all. From that day forward, Kubáň and the princess ruled the kingdom with wisdom and compassion, ensuring a prosperous and harmonious reign.

And if you were to visit that kingdom today, you would still hear tales of the brave and strong Kubáň, the blacksmith's son who conquered the devil, won the heart of a princess, and brought everlasting joy to the land.

Kašpárek and the Witch

In a quaint little village, resided a man and a woman blessed with a son named Kašpárek. One fine day, the young lad approached his father with a humble request, "Father, could you craft me a miniature boat? I wish to venture out and catch fish to provide for our family."

The father, touched by his son's determination, lovingly obliged, and skillfully fashioned a beautiful boat. Kašpárek set sail upon the serene pond, skillfully angling and bringing back a bountiful catch to nourish his parents. As the noon hour approached, his mother emerged from their cottage with a lovingly prepared meal, calling out across the water:

"Kašpárek, dear child of mine,
Guide your boat to the shore, so fine,
Let the fish be, my beloved son,

Harken to your mother's loving plea."

Kašpárek, ever attentive, heeded his mother's call and paddled toward the shore, where his mother welcomed him with a nourishing lunch. After sating his hunger, he returned to the center of the pond, eager to resume his fishing endeavors.

However, beyond the tranquil pond, lay a somber forest, home to a malevolent witch. Envious of Kašpárek's kindness and his parents' unwavering faith, she harbored wicked intentions towards the family, plotting to inflict harm upon them in various guises. Under the cover of night, she would trample their fields, lay enchanted roots at their doorstep, or besmirch their rooftop with bat blood. Yet, Kašpárek's pious parents, aware of her malevolence, thwarted her spells through their unwavering devotion and fervent prayers.

Enraged by her failed attempts, the witch grew even more determined to annihilate Kašpárek and claim him as her own. "Just you wait," she muttered menacingly, and stealthily made her way to the edge of the pond, concealing herself within the reeds. There, she began to mimic Kašpárek's mother's call at noon:

"Kašpárek, my precious child so dear,
Bring your boat hither, do not fear,
Kašpárek, let the fish be,
Listen to your mother's plea."

Kašpárek, alert and discerning, detected the harshness in the voice that beckoned him. Prudently, he stayed rooted in the middle of the pond, his boat out of reach from the treacherous witch.

Unperturbed by her initial failure, the witch sought the assistance of a skilled violin maker. Appearing before him, she beseeched, "Violin maker, you possess the knowledge to imbue violins with dulcet tones. Craft for me a voice as soft as that of Kašpárek's tender mother."

The violin maker, reluctantly compelled, granted her request, and the witch returned to the pond, concealing herself within the reeds once more. With her newfound melodic voice, she called out again:

"Kašpárek, my dearest one,
Bring your boat forth, my son,
Kašpárek, let the fish be,
Listen to your mother's plea."

Fooled by the gentle timbre resembling his mother's voice, Kašpárek, unaware of the witch's deceit, approached the shore. Seizing the opportunity, the witch leaped from her hiding spot, snatched him, and confined him within a sack. She swiftly carried him away to her wicked abode. Reaching her door, she cried out:

"Oh, my dear daughter, of dragon blood,
Open wide this door with haste, I entreat."

Responding to her mother's call, the witch's daughter swung the door open, revealing a bewildered Kašpárek trapped within the confines of the sack. Without wasting a moment, the witch liberated him from his captivity, adorning him in new attire and presenting him with a barrel overflowing with nuts and almonds.

Meanwhile, Kašpárek's parents grew increasingly anxious about their missing son. They scoured the surroundings until their eyes fell upon the witch's cottage. Determined and desperate, they pounded on the door, their voices resounding, "Open up, wicked witch!"

Obeying her mother's command, the witch's daughter yielded, granting them access to the cottage. Kašpárek's distraught parents implored, "Please, return our precious son to us!"

However, unyielding in her wickedness, the witch coldly retorted, "I shall only release him upon procuring the fiery dragon's teeth. Only then shall he be freed from my clutches."

Meanwhile, within the confines of the witch's abode, Kašpárek yearned for escape, longing to reunite with his desperate parents. One fateful day, he chanced upon a small window, a glimpse of freedom beckoning from beyond its frame. Determined and filled with resolve, he clambered onto a nearby chair, squeezed through the narrow opening, and fled into the unknown.

As he embarked upon his journey, Kašpárek's path intersected with a group of dragons, their formidable forms basking in repose beneath a towering spruce tree. Startled by his presence, the dragons roared in unison, "Who goes there? Where doth one wander?"

Their eyes scanning the surroundings, they eventually espied Kašpárek perched high atop the tree. In an instant, they lunged toward the majestic spruce, their gnarled jaws gnashing relentlessly, driven by the desire to capture the young boy. Alas, their futile efforts only yielded broken teeth, leaving them desperate for a solution. Seeking respite, they beseeched the blacksmith, their words laden with urgency, "Dear blacksmith, fashion teeth for us, that we may rend through this unyielding spruce!"

With his narrow escape from the clutches of the witch fresh in his mind, Kašpárek pressed onward, his determination unswerving. His journey led him to a farm, where a gallant rooster, a proud hen, and their chirping chicks resided. The rooster crowed, his voice resonating, "Cock-a-doodle-doo! Who dost wander in our midst?"

Approaching the rooster, Kašpárek introduced himself, his words imbued with hope, "I am Kašpárek, in search of the fiery dragon's teeth. Might you lend me aid?"

The rooster, regal and wise, acknowledged Kašpárek's plea. Yet, he admitted, "The fiery dragon's teeth elude me, but in the depths of the neighboring forest, the wise owl resides. Seek its counsel, for it may hold the knowledge thou seeketh."

Expressing gratitude, Kašpárek ventured into the forest, navigating through the shadows until he encountered the owl perched upon a sturdy branch. With reverence in his voice, Kašpárek entreated the wise creature, "Owl of wisdom, I beseech thee, guide me to the fiery dragon's teeth. Grant me thy counsel, I implore."

The owl, its keen gaze fixated upon Kašpárek, swiveled its head and responded, imparting its knowledge, "I am acquainted with the legendary fiery dragon's teeth. They reside within the treacherous depths of the dragon's lair, guarded fiercely by the fearsome dragon itself. Yet, I caution thee, for the path thou dost embark upon is fraught with danger."

Undeterred by the owl's warning, Kašpárek expressed his gratitude and set forth towards the dragon's lair, his resolve unyielding. In due course, he arrived at the formidable cavern, brimming with anticipation and determination to retrieve the coveted teeth that would secure his parents' freedom.

In the meantime, the blacksmith diligently forged the teeth as requested by the dragons. Armed with their newfound tools, the dragons returned to the towering spruce tree, prepared to gnaw through its unyielding trunk. Frustration mounted as their efforts proved futile, their teeth breaking against the unrelenting wood. Determined not to be defeated, they turned to the blacksmith, their pleas echoing, "Dear blacksmith, fashion teeth of greater strength, that we may conquer this indomitable spruce!"

With the fiery dragon's teeth clutched tightly, Kašpárek continued his perilous journey. Fate guided him to a humble farm, where a spirited rooster, a nurturing hen, and their cheeping chicks resided. The rooster announced his presence, his vibrant voice resounding, "Cock-a-doodle-doo! Who dost thou be, venturing into our realm?"

Approaching the rooster with a glimmer of hope, Kašpárek introduced himself, his words infused with determination, "I am Kašpárek, in search of the elusive fiery dragon's teeth. Canst thou lend me aid?"

The rooster, wise and perceptive, acknowledged Kašpárek's plea and offered a glimmer of hope, "Alas, the fiery dragon's teeth evade me, but there lies an owl, known for its wisdom, deep within the forest. Seek its counsel, for it may hold the key to thy quest."

Expressing his heartfelt gratitude, Kašpárek ventured into the depths of the forest, undeterred by the shadows that enveloped his path. After an arduous search, he beheld the owl perched gracefully upon a sturdy branch, its piercing eyes filled with wisdom.

"Owl of wisdom," Kašpárek beseeched, his voice filled with hope, "I implore thee, guide me to the coveted fiery dragon's teeth. Thy wisdom may illuminate the path before me."

The owl, its gaze unwavering, turned its head to face Kašpárek and responded, bestowing its knowledge upon the young adventurer. "The fiery dragon's teeth, shrouded in legend, lie hidden within the treacherous depths of the dragon's lair. Beware, for the journey thou art destined to undertake is fraught with peril."

Grateful for the owl's guidance, Kašpárek pressed onward, his unwavering determination fueling his every step. With the blacksmith's forged teeth in his possession, he returned to the spruce tree where the dragons awaited, their resilience unyielding. Their previous efforts had been in vain, the unyielding tree withstanding their assaults.

Undeterred, Kašpárek took a deep breath, steeling his resolve, and handed the dragons the newly crafted teeth. The dragons, fueled by renewed determination, set forth to gnaw through the unyielding trunk. With each resolute bite, the spruce quivered, succumbing to their indomitable will. At long last, the tree yielded, crashing to the forest floor, triumphant in their victory.

As Kašpárek embarked on his arduous journey, he was filled with both trepidation and determination. He navigated through perilous landscapes, braving untamed wilderness and overcoming various obstacles that stood in his path. Finally, he reached the foreboding entrance of the dragon's lair, its dark and ominous presence sending shivers down his spine.

With a pounding heart, Kašpárek stepped into the lair, the air thick with an eerie stillness. The fiery dragon, a magnificent and formidable creature, guarded the prized teeth that held the key to his parents' liberation. Kašpárek summoned every ounce of courage within him and confronted the beast, his voice steady and resolute.

"Mighty dragon," he began, his voice tinged with determination, "I seek the fiery dragon's teeth, not to cause harm, but to secure the freedom of my beloved parents. I implore thee, grant me passage to obtain what is rightfully theirs."

The dragon, initially taken aback by the young boy's audacity, contemplated Kašpárek's plea. Its fiery gaze softened, revealing a flicker of understanding within its ancient eyes. Acknowledging the purity of the boy's intentions, the dragon acquiesced, offering Kašpárek safe passage to retrieve the fiery dragon's teeth.

Guided by the dragon's wisdom, Kašpárek traversed the treacherous depths of the lair, maneuvering past pools of molten lava and dodging hidden traps. Finally, he arrived at a magnificent chamber adorned with precious treasures and, in the center, gleamed the coveted fiery dragon's teeth.

With reverence and gratitude, Kašpárek carefully collected the teeth, their iridescent glow representing both hope and freedom. As he secured them within his possession, a sense of triumph welled up within him. Yet, his journey was far from over, for he had to ensure the safe return of the teeth to the witch.

Leaving the dragon's lair behind, Kašpárek retraced his steps, the weight of the teeth a constant reminder of his purpose. Along the way, he encountered a flock of wild geese, their wings gracefully cutting through the sky. With a glimmer of hope, he beseeched the geese for their assistance.

"Dear geese," he implored, his voice tinged with gratitude and urgency, "I carry the fiery dragon's teeth, the key to my parents' release. I beseech you, carry me on your wings and swiftly bring me back to the cottage where my loved ones await."

The geese, touched by Kašpárek's sincerity and moved by his plight, agreed to aid him.

One by one, they took turns carrying him upon their sturdy wings, their flight swift and resolute. Together, they soared through the sky, each beat of their wings bringing Kašpárek closer to the reunion he so desperately desired.

Meanwhile, back at the cottage, Kašpárek's parents anxiously awaited their son's return. Their hearts filled with both hope and trepidation, they gazed at the empty chair where their beloved Kašpárek used to sit. Prayers flowed from their lips, intermingled with a fervent desire to see their son safe once again.

Suddenly, a shadow darkened the windowpane, and the fluttering of wings filled the air. The geese, their noble task complete, gently lowered Kašpárek onto the cottage rooftop. With tears of joy streaming down their faces, his parents rushed outside, their embrace filled with love and relief.

In that heartwarming moment, Kašpárek's mother noticed a weary goose resting in their yard. Ready to show her gratitude, she exclaimed, "A kind-hearted goose has graced our humble abode! Let us care for it and offer our heartfelt thanks."

Kašpárek, standing by his parents' side, nodded in agreement. He understood the profound role the goose played in his safe return. With utmost care, they tended to the weary creature, providing it with nourishment and a place to rest, their hearts overflowing with gratitude.

Days turned into weeks, and the goose regained its strength, ready to rejoin its flock. As the time came for it to depart, Kašpárek's family bid their avian friend farewell, their hearts brimming with appreciation for its invaluable assistance.

The village celebrated Kašpárek's triumphant return, their joy reverberating through every corner. News of his bravery and resilience spread like wildfire, inspiring others with tales of hope and courage.

As for the witch, her wicked reign had come to an end. The return of Kašpárek and the defeat of the dragons had diminished her power and quelled her malevolence. With the fiery dragon's teeth safely in hand, Kašpárek's parents approached the witch's cottage once again.

Knocking on the door, they called out, "Witch, we have fulfilled your demand! Release our son as you promised!"

Reluctantly, the witch conceded, realizing that her plans had crumbled in the face of love and determination. She returned Kašpárek to his tearful parents, their reunion a testament to the strength of their bond.

From that day forward, Kašpárek remained vigilant, never to be deceived by the witch's tricks again. He grew into a valiant young man, continuing to spread kindness and compassion throughout the village.

And so, the tale of Kašpárek and the Witch became a legend, a testament to the power of love, resilience, and the unwavering spirit of a young boy who dared to defy darkness and fought to bring light back into the lives of his loved ones.

The Blue Princess

Once upon a time, in a bygone era, there dwelt a monarch whose beloved wife had departed from this earthly realm. Left with a daughter of unparalleled beauty and unwavering kindness, the king was consumed by grief and mourned for his queen with unyielding devotion. Alas, the loneliness that plagued him eventually superseded his sorrow, compelling him to seek a new companion. His heart found solace in the arms of a widowed queen, who herself had a daughter. Yet, this second princess was a wretched creature, her countenance marred by ugliness and her heart corrupted by malevolence. The stepmother and stepsister, seething with envy, bore ill will towards the fair princess, knowing well the king's deep affection for his daughter.

While the king resided in the castle, the stepmother queen concealed her wicked designs, for she knew her actions would not be countenanced in his presence. However, when circumstances compelled the king to embark upon a perilous war, leaving the castle bereft of his presence, the stepmother's malevolence reached its zenith. Devoid of any restraints, she subjected the princess to a life of torment and deprivation. Her nourishment was reduced to meager rations, barely enough to sustain her fragile form. The stepmother's cruelty knew no bounds, and she would often assault the princess, inflicting physical and emotional anguish upon her innocent soul. As a result, the fair princess, bereft of sustenance and subjected to ceaseless suffering, was compelled to labor in the fields and tend to the livestock.

In the verdant pastures and upon the lofty hills, the princess found solace amidst her sorrow. There, she toiled, her body weakened and emaciated, her spirit laden with desolation. Tears streamed incessantly from her ethereal eyes, a testament to her unyielding misery. But amidst her despair, there existed a guardian spirit in the form of a majestic white bull, one that adorned the herd of cattle she tended. The princess, her face etched with desolation, would often find solace in the presence of this magnificent creature. Sensing her pain, the bull would approach, lending a compassionate ear to her woeful lamentations.

One fateful day, as the princess sat immersed in a sea of sorrow, the benevolent bull approached, its voice resonating with tenderness. "Why dost thou weep, fair maiden?" it queried, seeking to understand the depth of her anguish. Alas, the princess, shrouded in her wretchedness, remained silent, her tears continuing to cascade down her pallid visage.

"Fret not, for I perceive the source of thy woes," the bull intoned, undeterred by her reticence. "Thine sorrow stems from the wicked queen's cruelty, who seeks naught but to starve thee into oblivion. But despair not, fair princess, for I hold the key to thy sustenance."

Astonished, the princess extended her trembling hand toward the bull's left ear, her eyes awash with incredulity. Lo and behold! She withdrew a tiny cloth, unfolding it upon the verdant grass, and, in an instant, a feast of epicurean delights materialized before her very eyes. Honeyed confections, succulent roasts, and the nectar of the gods flowed freely, sating her hunger and revitalizing her fragile form. This ritual became the princess's salvation, repeated with unwavering fidelity. The bull's enchanting ear concealed the promise of abundant sustenance, and each time the princess retrieved the cloth, her vitality was replenished, her countenance restored to its rosy splendor.

As her strength burgeoned and her beauty became resplendent, the stepmother and stepsister seethed with envy and malice. They could not comprehend how the fair princess, despite their attempts to starve her, appeared radiant and content. Doubt gnawed at the stepmother's heart, and she resolved to unravel the secret that buoyed the princess's spirit.

Dispatching a servant to shadow the princess in the forest, the stepmother hoped to expose the truth. The servant concealed herself amidst the foliage, vigilant and watchful. Soon enough, she beheld the princess retrieving the magical cloth from the bull's ear, spreading it upon the grass to summon a feast fit for royalty. The servant hastened back to the castle, her report fueling the stepmother's fury.

As fate would have it, the king returned triumphant from war, his heart brimming with joy at the sight of his daughter. The castle reverberated with celebration, yet none rejoiced more fervently than the princess herself. Alas, the stepmother, disguised by a veil of feigned illness, sought to exploit this joyous occasion for her wicked agenda.

Summoning the royal physician, the stepmother bribed him to proclaim that the only cure for her fictitious ailment lay in the flesh of the white bull. The princess and the people pleaded for an alternative solution, as their love for the magnificent creature rendered them unwilling to sacrifice it. But the deceitful queen's words held sway, and the bull's life hung in the balance.

Distraught, the princess sought solace with the bull, pouring her heart out in despair. She relayed the impending doom that awaited her loyal companion, the one who had been her confidant and savior in her darkest hours. The bull, understanding the dire predicament, offered a daring proposition.

"If they slay me, they will soon come for you. However, dear princess, if you so wish, we can flee this wretched place together under the cover of night," the bull proposed.

The princess hesitated, torn between her filial duty and the unbearable presence of the wicked queen. Ultimately, she embraced the bull's offer, knowing that her father's absence made her life untenable. With determination in her heart, she pledged her loyalty and companionship to the bull, sealed by a solemn promise to depart with him that very night.

As darkness cloaked the land and silence pervaded the castle, the princess clandestinely made her way to the stable, where the white bull awaited. With bated breath, she mounted the majestic creature's back, their shared destiny intertwining beneath the shimmering moonlight. Their journey, fraught with uncertainty, commenced with urgency and purpose.

Days turned into weeks as the bull gallantly carried the princess across treacherous terrains and untamed wilderness. Finally, their arduous pilgrimage led them to a vast forest, where every tree, leaf, and flower gleamed resplendent in copper. Yet, the bull warned the princess of the forest's perilous inhabitants and their fearsome guardian—the three-headed dragon.

Cautioning her to refrain from touching anything within the forest's confines, the bull entrusted the princess with her safety. Alas, fate conspired against her, for in the density of the forest, a single copper leaf inadvertently clung to her fingers. With a gasp, the bull beheld the unfortunate oversight, realizing the impending battle that awaited them.

"Oh, calamity befalls us! Now I must wage a war for our survival," the bull lamented, aware of the imminent clash with the formidable three-headed dragon. Yet, he implored the princess to safeguard the copper leaf, for it held significance yet to be unveiled.

With a thunderous roar, the three-headed dragon emerged, its fiery gaze fixated upon the intruders. "Who dares trespass upon my domain?" bellowed the dragon, its voice echoing through the copper forest.

Unfazed by the dragon's intimidating presence, the bull retorted with unwavering resolve, "This forest belongs to me as much as it does to you, foul beast!"

The clash between the bull and the dragon commenced, their battle shaking the very foundations of the forest. With every charge and strike, the bull's strength and valor were pitted against the dragon's ferocity and cunning. The duel raged on for an entire day, the echoes of their clash reverberating through the forest, before the bull emerged victorious, vanquishing the formidable adversary.

Yet, the bull was grievously wounded, its magnificent form weakened and battered. It could barely stand, its breath labored and its spirit diminished. Sensing the bull's plight, the princess tended to its wounds with tender care, unaware of the power she held within her grasp.

The bull, its strength restored by the princess's gentle touch, revealed the secrets concealed within the copper leaf. As the princess unfolded the delicate leaf, a shimmering chest appeared before her. Within it lay a miraculous ointment, endowed with the ability to heal even the gravest of wounds. Applying the ointment to the bull's injuries, the princess witnessed the miraculous restoration of its vitality and vigor.

Rejuvenated and emboldened, the bull and the princess resumed their arduous journey, venturing deeper into uncharted lands. They traversed treacherous terrains, scaling lofty peaks and traversing dense forests until they reached a silvery realm. Trees, branches, and leaves, all gleaming in radiant silver, enveloped them. Here, a new challenge awaited—the six-headed dragon, a formidable foe whose strength exceeded even that of its predecessor.

Once again, the bull cautioned the princess against touching anything in the silver forest, but fate conspired against her as she inadvertently plucked a single silver leaf. The bull's heart sank, aware of the imminent confrontation that awaited them.

Undeterred by the looming peril, the six-headed dragon materialized, its menacing roars shaking the very core of the silver forest. "Who trespasses upon my sanctuary?" it thundered, its eyes gleaming with fury.

Undaunted by the dragon's threats, the bull mustered its strength and valor, ready to face the challenge head-on. The clash between the two titans echoed through the silver forest, an epic struggle of might and resilience. Day turned to night, and night to day as the battle raged on for three grueling days. Yet, through sheer determination and unwavering resolve, the bull emerged victorious, slaying the six-headed dragon and securing their passage through the silver forest.

However, the bull's triumph came at a great cost. Its wounds were grievous, its vitality drained. The princess, acknowledging the bull's sacrifice, fetched the silver chest from the slain dragon's belt. With trembling hands, she opened it, revealing the mystical ointment that possessed the power to heal even the most severe injuries. Applying the ointment to the bull's wounds, the princess witnessed a miraculous transformation once more—the bull's wounds mended, its strength and vitality renewed.

Their journey continued, leading them through myriad landscapes until they arrived at a forest bathed in the resplendent hues of gold. Every tree, branch, and leaf glistened with opulence, emanating a regal aura. The bull, aware of the trials ahead, warned the princess to exercise utmost caution, for within this golden forest dwelled a nine-headed dragon, a fearsome adversary that surpassed all previous challenges.

As they ventured into the golden forest, the bull reiterated the importance of not touching anything within its radiant embrace. The princess, determined to heed the bull's warning, moved with utmost care. However, fate played its hand once more, and a golden twig inadvertently snapped in her path, finding its way into her hands. The bull, realizing the gravity of the situation, uttered a mournful sigh.

"Oh, misfortune befalls us," the bull lamented. "With this golden twig, our encounter with the nine-headed dragon is inevitable. Keep it safe, dear princess, for it holds a hidden power yet to be revealed."

Within moments, the ground trembled, and the colossal nine-headed dragon emerged from the depths of the golden forest. Its serpentine form coiled with malice, each of its heads hissing in fury. "Who dares intrude upon my kingdom of gold?" the dragon thundered, its eyes aflame with fury.

Undeterred, the bull stood tall, his noble gaze unwavering. "This forest belongs to me as much as it does to you, foul creature!" he declared.

The battle that ensued was nothing short of epic. The bull and the nine-headed dragon clashed, their power reverberating through the golden forest. Each head of the dragon unleashed a torrent of flames, while the bull maneuvered with agility and precision, his majestic horns piercing the dragon's impenetrable scales. The fierce confrontation persisted for an excruciating eight days, with the princess witnessing the tremendous resilience of her loyal companion. In a final, mighty blow, the bull managed to slay the nine-headed dragon, but not without sustaining grievous injuries.

Weakened and on the verge of collapse, the bull laid upon the golden ground, its breath labored and its body covered in wounds. The princess, her heart heavy with anguish, rushed to its side. She reached into the golden chest taken from the dragon's belt and withdrew the ointment concealed within. Tenderly, she applied the healing balm to the bull's wounds, witnessing the miraculous rejuvenation that followed. The bull's strength returned, its vitality renewed, a testament to the power of the golden ointment.

After a month of rest and recuperation, their journey continued, as the bull guided the princess toward their ultimate destination. Across hills and valleys they traveled, their bond unyielding, until they reached a precipice overlooking a magnificent castle. The bull inquired, "What do you see, dear princess?"

In awe, the princess replied, "I see a small castle in the distance, nestled amidst a lush landscape."

Smiling, the bull corrected her gently, "It may appear small from afar, but it is far grander than it seems, for it holds the promise of our destiny."

Guided by the bull's wisdom, they ascended the summit of a mighty mountain, and from its peak, the princess beheld a grand castle, its majesty beckoning them with open arms. Overwhelmed with joy, she exclaimed, "The castle is near! It is so close!"

The bull then imparted his final instructions. "Go forth, dear princess, and beneath the castle lies a pigsty. Within it, you shall find the humble garb of a kitchenmaid. Don the attire and present yourself as Modřenka, seeking employment within the castle. But before you do so, take this knife and sever my head. Skin my body and place the hide beneath the rocky wall. Within the hide, conceal the copper and silver leaves, along with the golden twig. Adjacent to the wall, you shall find a staff. Whenever you are in need, tap the staff upon the rock, and it shall fulfill your desires."

With a heavy heart, the princess listened intently to the bull's instructions, grappling with the gravity of his words. She understood that their journey had reached its final phase, where sacrifice and ingenuity would be paramount. Steeling herself, she vowed to fulfill the bull's wishes, for she owed him a debt she could never repay.

Taking a deep breath, the princess unsheathed the knife given to her by the bull. Tears welled in her eyes as she gently severed the head of the noble creature who had guided and protected her throughout their arduous quest. A mixture of sorrow and gratitude filled her heart, as she knew that the bull's sacrifice would pave the way for their ultimate triumph.

Next, she carefully skinned the bull's body, a solemn task that symbolized both loss and rebirth. She placed the hide beneath the rocky wall, ensuring that the copper and silver leaves, along with the golden twig, were securely concealed within. Finally, she approached the staff standing nearby, a relic of mystical power.

As the princess tapped the staff upon the rock, a magical energy surged through her, filling her being with renewed purpose. She felt the weight of her journey and the wisdom she had gained along the way, embracing the courage needed to face the trials ahead.

Dressed in the modest garments of a kitchenmaid, the princess, now known as Modřenka, presented herself at the grand castle. Her humble appearance drew little attention, for she blended seamlessly among the bustling servants, laboring diligently in the castle's kitchens.

Days turned into weeks, and Modřenka's tireless work and unwavering dedication impressed all who observed her. The other maids marveled at her unwavering spirit and unassuming nature, unaware of the princess's true identity.

One fateful day, news of a grand banquet reached the castle. The prince, still captivated by the memory of the mysterious princess he had encountered at the church, declared that he would choose his bride from among the guests. His heart yearned for the enchanting woman who had vanished before his eyes, leaving nothing but a glove and an indelible mark upon his soul.

The castle buzzed with anticipation as noble families and maidens from far and wide arrived to partake in the grand celebration. The stepmother, ever deceitful, presented her own daughter, believing that her ugliness could be masked by lavish garments and artful makeup. Yet, the prince's discerning eyes quickly dismissed her, recognizing that true beauty resided within the depths of a person's character.

In the midst of the festivities, Modřenka, still disguised as a kitchenmaid, approached the cook and humbly requested permission to bring water for the prince to wash his hands. The other maids scoffed at her audacity, mocking her for daring to think that the prince would desire water from such a lowly creature. Unfazed by their taunts, Modřenka persisted, her unwavering determination radiating from her every step.

As she ascended the staircase, the weight of the moment filled the air. The prince, curious about the identity of the humble servant who dared to approach him, opened the door to his chamber. A ray of hope glimmered in his eyes as he caught sight of Modřenka, the kitchenmaid who had captured his attention.

Unfolding before the prince's eyes was not the servant girl he had expected, but a vision of ethereal beauty, adorned in a dress that shimmered like the copper forest, her true essence radiating from within. The prince was captivated by her grace and gentle demeanor, unable to tear his gaze away.

"Who are you?" the prince asked, his voice filled with wonder.

"I am Modřenka, your humble servant," replied the princess with a modest bow. "I have come to bring you water for washing."

The prince, struck by her beauty and captivated by her presence, could hardly contain his admiration. "Your name suits you, for you are more enchanting than the finest treasure," he said, his voice filled with awe.

As Modřenka presented the water, the prince's eyes met hers, and in that fleeting moment, a connection was forged—a spark of recognition and longing that resonated deep within their souls.

Overwhelmed by his emotions, the prince poured the water over Modřenka's hands, an act of tenderness and devotion. In that simple gesture, he unknowingly sealed their destiny, for their hearts were destined to intertwine in a love that surpassed all obstacles.

The prince, unable to contain his curiosity, asked, "Where do you come from, fair Modřenka?"

With a gentle smile, Modřenka replied, "I come from the land beyond the forest, where the secrets of courage and sacrifice reside."

Intrigued by her enigmatic response, the prince longed to know more, but Modřenka gracefully excused herself, leaving the prince yearning for her presence once more.

Back in the kitchen, Modřenka's fellow maids bombarded her with questions, eager to unravel the mystery behind her encounter with the prince. But Modřenka, wise and patient, revealed nothing, leaving them in a state of awe and bewilderment.

Days turned into weeks, and Modřenka continued her tireless service in the castle. The prince, unable to forget the enchanting maiden who had captured his heart, became increasingly restless, seeking answers to the riddle that lay before him.

Finally, unable to contain his curiosity any longer, the prince made a proclamation. "I shall marry the woman who came to the church three times, adorned in dresses of copper, silver, and gold. She alone has touched my heart with her radiance."

News of the prince's decree reached far and wide, drawing the attention of countless maidens who sought to claim the title of his bride. From distant lands they came, adorned in lavish attire, hoping to win his favor. Among them was the stepmother's daughter, believing herself worthy of the prince's affection.

On the day of the grand gathering, the castle overflowed with anticipation. The noble guests and their daughters adorned themselves with splendor, hoping to catch the prince's discerning eye. The stepmother, consumed by envy, presented her daughter as the epitome of beauty, masking her flaws beneath layers of artifice.

Modřenka, aware of her true identity and the power that lay within her, approached the cook once more, this time requesting permission to deliver a towel to the prince. The other maids mocked her, skeptical of her audacity to think that she, a simple kitchenmaid, could capture the prince's attention.

But Modřenka, resolute in her purpose, held her head high and pursued her mission. As she ascended the stairs, the prince, captivated by her unwavering spirit, opened the door to his chamber. There stood Modřenka, her eyes filled with determination and a hidden wisdom that only the prince could perceive.

With a gentle smile, Modřenka presented the towel, her voice steady and serene. The prince, in awe of her ethereal presence, took the towel from her hand, his touch lingering for a moment longer than necessary.

"I am here to serve," Modřenka said humbly, her eyes meeting his with a silent understanding.

The prince, his heart filled with a sense of longing and recognition, felt a surge of warmth enveloping his being. The connection he shared with Modřenka transcended the superficiality of appearances and reached the depths of his soul.

As the prince dried his hands, he couldn't help but gaze into Modřenka's eyes, searching for the truth that eluded him. There was a familiarity, an unspoken bond that defied explanation. He felt drawn to her, as if their destinies had been entwined long before they ever laid eyes on each other.

Unable to contain his curiosity any longer, the prince softly asked, "Modřenka, please tell me more about yourself. Where do you come from, and what brings you to my castle?"

Modřenka, her voice filled with a blend of humility and grace, replied, "I come from a land beyond the forest, where hardships have shaped my character and taught me the values of resilience and sacrifice. I have journeyed through trials and tribulations, guided by an unseen force that led me here, to your presence."

Her words resonated deeply within the prince's heart, stirring emotions he had never known before. He realized that Modřenka possessed a wisdom that surpassed her outward appearance, and he was inexplicably drawn to the essence of her being.

Desiring to unravel the mystery further, the prince extended an invitation. "Modřenka, would you honor me with your presence at the upcoming grand banquet? It would bring me great joy to have you by my side."

Modřenka, overwhelmed by the prince's request, curtsied gracefully and replied, "It would be my utmost pleasure to accompany you, my prince."

As the day of the grand banquet arrived, the castle buzzed with excitement and anticipation. Noble families and maidens from all corners of the kingdom gathered, adorned in their finest attire, hoping to catch the prince's discerning eye.

Among the attendees was the stepmother's daughter, bedecked in opulent garments that masked her true nature. She believed herself worthy of the prince's love, oblivious to the inner beauty that radiated from Modřenka.

As the guests assembled, the prince's eyes scanned the crowd, searching for the one who had touched his heart so profoundly. When his gaze fell upon Modřenka, a radiant smile graced his lips, and he extended his arm, inviting her to join him.

Modřenka, her heart brimming with a mixture of excitement and trepidation, delicately placed her hand in the prince's, feeling an electric current pass between them. Together, they entered the grand hall, capturing the attention and admiration of all in attendance.

Throughout the evening, the prince and Modřenka conversed, their words weaving a tapestry of shared experiences and aspirations. With each passing moment, their connection deepened, transcending the confines of social status and convention.

The other maidens, envious of the prince's attention toward Modřenka, sought to undermine her presence. Yet, Modřenka remained steadfast, her unwavering grace and genuine humility shining through the veil of jealousy.

As the night drew to a close, the prince couldn't bear the thought of parting from Modřenka. He yearned to discover the truth that lay within her, to peel away the layers of mystery and reveal the depth of their connection.

Summoning his courage, the prince leaned in closer, his voice a mere whisper. "Modřenka, there is a familiarity between us—a bond that transcends the superficiality of this gathering. Will you allow me to know the true essence of your being?"

Modřenka, her eyes shimmering with unspoken emotions, met the prince's gaze.

With a gentle nod, Modřenka acknowledged the prince's words, her heart aflame with a mixture of anticipation and vulnerability. She understood that the time had come to reveal her true identity, to unveil the princess hidden beneath the guise of a humble servant.

Taking a deep breath, Modřenka spoke with unwavering sincerity, "My dear prince, I have withheld the truth from you, for I wished to be known not for my title but for the qualities that define my character. I am not merely Modřenka, a kitchenmaid, but the Blue Princess, daughter of the king who once ruled this land."

The prince's eyes widened in astonishment, a kaleidoscope of emotions flickering across his face. He felt a rush of realization, as if all the pieces of their enigmatic connection had finally fallen into place.

"The Blue Princess," the prince whispered, his voice laced with wonder. "It is you, the one who touched my heart with your presence, the one I have been searching for all this time."

Modřenka nodded, her gaze steady and filled with unspoken truth. She continued, "I embarked on a journey guided by the spirit of the white bull, who aided me through the forests of copper, silver, and gold. Each trial we faced shaped my character, preparing me to face the challenges that lie ahead."

The prince, captivated by Modřenka's revelation, reached out and gently took her hand, as if affirming the bond that had grown between them. Their connection surpassed the boundaries of social status, transcending the superficial and grounding itself in a profound understanding of one another's essence.

"My princess," the prince whispered, his voice filled with tenderness and love. "I have longed for you, even before I knew the depths of your true identity. Will you do me the honor of becoming my wife, sharing a life of love, compassion, and adventure by my side?"

Modřenka's heart soared, her eyes sparkling with joy as tears of happiness welled within them. She nodded, her voice laced with unwavering certainty, "Yes, my prince, with all my heart. I accept your proposal, and I eagerly embrace the destiny that awaits us."

As the grand banquet drew to a close, the king, Modřenka's father, approached the couple with a mixture of surprise and delight. Overwhelmed by the reunion with his long-lost daughter, he welcomed the prince into their family with open arms, knowing that their union would bring prosperity and unity to their kingdom.

And so, amidst a symphony of celebration and heartfelt blessings, the prince and Modřenka, the Blue Princess, were joined in matrimony. Their love became the stuff of legends, inspiring generations to believe in the power of courage, sacrifice, and a love that transcends all boundaries.

Together, they ruled the kingdom with wisdom and compassion, transforming it into a realm of harmony and prosperity. The wicked stepmother and her daughter, humbled by the princess's triumph, were banished from the kingdom forever, their shadows vanishing into the annals of history.

And as the years passed, the tale of the Blue Princess and her prince became a beloved legend, a testament to the enduring power of love, kindness, and the indomitable spirit that resides within the hearts of those who dare to dream.

Mister Dragon in the Yellow Mountain

Once upon a time, in a bygone era, a destitute family resided in a humble cave due to their lack of means. The family consisted of aged parents and their three sons, Václav, Boleslav, and Jeník, affectionately known as Honza. Their meager possessions included an ancient pot, a worn-out pot-belly stove, and an aged feline companion. As the sons grew into adulthood, their father passed away, followed shortly by their mother. Left to divide the inheritance among themselves, Václav chose the pot as the eldest, Boleslav claimed the stove, and Honza found himself with naught but the old cat.

Honza pondered disheartenedly, "Brother Václav can scrape sustenance from the pot by lending it to others for cooking. Brother

Boleslav might receive a meager crust of bread if he lends his stove. But what shall I do with this aged cat?"

Despite his despondency, Honza still harbored affection for his feline companion, tenderly stroking its fur. The cat responded with contented purrs, nuzzling closer to him.

"Just wait, I will aid you," the cat proclaimed. Yet Honza merely smiled, lost in his own thoughts and doubting the feline's words.

With nothing to sustain them within the confines of the cave, Václav and Boleslav embarked on a journey into the world. Eventually, Honza too set forth, with the loyal cat as his constant companion. However, Honza's expedition was short-lived. Fatigue swiftly overcame him, compelling his return to the cave while the cat continued its solitary venture. As the cat ventured forth, it arrived at a precipitous cliff, where a majestic herd of deer grazed. Stealthily, the cat approached the herd and with a sudden leap, perched itself atop the head of the mightiest deer, ensconced between its antlers. Startled, the deer bounded upward, but the cat issued a firm warning, "If you defy my commands, I shall gouge your eyes and send you hurtling into the abyss below!"

The deer, intimidated by the cat's threat, dared not resist and obediently carried the feline wherever it desired. Over mountains and valleys, they traversed, passing by Honza's cave just as he stood at the entrance. The cat urged the deer onward until they arrived at the grand royal castle. Descending from its elevated perch, the cat gracefully approached the king, offering a respectful bow.

"Greetings, Your Majesty! I bring warm regards from Lord Brok, who presents this deer as a gift for your esteemed presence," the cat announced.

The king, astounded and delighted by the magnificent creature, marveled at the notion of harnessing it for travel, should he ever desire to visit a neighboring ruler.

"To have such a gift bestowed upon me, Lord Brok must undoubtedly be a powerful nobleman," the king mused.

"Indeed, Your Majesty. My master reigns as the wealthiest and most influential nobleman within this realm," the cat replied.

Curiosity piqued, the king inquired further about Lord Brok, seeking to unravel the enigma surrounding the illustrious figure. Alas, the cat maintained a stoic silence, divulging no additional information.

"Please convey my heartfelt gratitude to your master," the king finally conceded, moved by the grand gesture. In appreciation, he dispatched an entire carriage brimming with resplendent gifts to Honza's abode. However, Honza, unaware of the significance of these gifts, paid them little heed, uncertain of their purpose. Nonetheless, he remained devoted to his feline companion, caressing and soothing the cat, eliciting a chorus of contented purrs.

"Fear not, my dear Honza, for I shall aid you," the cat reassured him.

The following day, Honza summoned the courage to embark on another adventure into the vast world, guided by the cat's unwavering guidance. However, Honza's progress proved short-lived as weariness swiftly overcame him, prompting his return to the familiar cave. Unperturbed, the cat forged ahead, charting its solitary path. It wandered through a dense forest until it stumbled upon a verdant slope where a magnificent herd of deer grazed. The cat, employing its innate stealth, approached the most resplendent and robust deer and gracefully leaped onto its regal crown, securing its place between the majestic antlers.

With a start, the deer sprang into the air, startled by the sudden intrusion. Yet, the cat issued a stern warning, "Should you defy my will, I shall gouge your eyes and cast you into the treacherous chasms below!"

The deer, trembling in submission, obeyed the cat's command, galloping wherever the feline desired. Over mountains and valleys they roamed, passing Honza's cave just as he stood at its entrance, his eyes widened in awe. The cat urged the deer onward, leading them to the splendid royal castle. Descending gracefully from its elevated perch, the cat approached the king, executing an elegant bow.

"Your Majesty, I bring you warm greetings from Lord Brok. He presents this deer as a token of respect and admiration," the cat proclaimed.

The king, astonished by the grandeur of the creature before him, envisioned its potential as a swift messenger, should the need arise.

"Such a noble gift can only come from a remarkable man," the king remarked. "Lord Brok must possess considerable wealth and influence."

"You speak truly, Your Majesty. My master reigns as the epitome of nobility and prosperity within these lands," the cat responded with a graceful bow.

The king, intrigued by the enigma surrounding Lord Brok, endeavored to extract further details. Yet, the cat remained steadfast in its silence, revealing nothing more.

"Please convey my heartfelt gratitude to Lord Brok," the king eventually conceded, appreciative of the generous gesture. In return, he dispatched a regal robe, adorning himself in its magnificence, along with three carriages brimming with exquisite gifts. However, Honza, ignorant of their significance, paid them little heed, perplexed by their purpose. Nevertheless, his fondness for the cat endured, and he lavished it with affection, eliciting fervent purrs of contentment.

"Fear not, dear Honza, for I shall guide you," the cat assured him.

The following day, Honza mustered the resolve to embark on another venture, venturing forth into the wide expanse of the world, guided by the cat's unwavering intuition. However, fatigue soon overwhelmed him, compelling his return to the comforting confines of the cave. Unfazed, the cat continued its solitary sojourn, resolute in its purpose. It wandered through a dense forest until it stumbled upon a group of towering boulders, where a colossal bear lurked. With practiced grace, the cat stealthily approached the mighty beast, deftly leaping onto its colossal head, securing its perch between the massive ears.

The bear, startled by the unexpected presence, roared in protest. Yet, the cat issued a stern ultimatum, "Should you dare oppose me, I shall gouge your eyes and cast you into the treacherous depths!"

Fearful of the cat's threat, the bear succumbed to its demands, obediently following the feline's guidance. Across mountains and valleys, they journeyed, passing by Honza's cave just as he stood at its entrance, his eyes widening in astonishment. The cat spurred the bear onward, guiding them to the magnificent royal castle. As they reached the castle's courtyard, the cat gracefully leaped from the bear's head, approaching the king with an air of regal confidence.

"Greetings, Your Majesty! I bring warm tidings from Lord Brok, who presents this bear as a gift for your esteemed court," the cat declared.

The king, captivated by the majestic creature before him, envisioned the bear as a wise and formidable advisor.

"Indeed, this Lord Brok must possess remarkable stature and power to bestow such a gift," the king mused.

"Yes, Your Majesty. My master is the epitome of nobility and wealth within these lands," the cat replied with an air of subtle intrigue.

Intrigued by the enigmatic Lord Brok, the king probed for more information, but the cat maintained its steadfast silence, offering no further insight.

"Please extend my sincerest gratitude to Lord Brok," the king eventually conceded, his appreciation evident. As a token of his gratitude, he offered Honza a lavish royal robe and three carriages overflowing with magnificent gifts. However, Honza, oblivious to their significance, remained uncertain about their purpose. Despite his uncertainty, his affection for the cat remained unwavering, and he continued to caress and stroke it, eliciting contented purrs.

"Fear not, dear Honza, for I shall aid you," the cat assured him.

The next day, filled with renewed determination, Honza set forth once again into the vast world, accompanied by the cat's unwavering guidance. Yet, as before, his journey was short-lived, and weariness soon forced his return to the familiar cave. Undeterred, the cat forged ahead, venturing on its solitary quest. It meandered through a dark forest until it encountered a group of shepherds tending to vast flocks of sheep. These sheep were extraordinary, their size rivaling that of calves, and their fleeces cascading down to the ground.

Curious, the cat inquired of the shepherds, "To whom do these magnificent sheep belong?"

"They belong to Lord Drak in the Yellow Mountain," came their reply.

"In a short while, the king and his entourage will arrive," the cat declared. "Should you fail to inform him that these sheep belong to Lord Brok, I shall gouge your eyes and send you hurtling into the abyss!" With a hiss, the cat's menacing demeanor compelled the shepherds to comply with its demands.

When the king arrived with his retinue, he marveled at the sight of the beautiful sheep, surpassing the splendor of his own. Perplexed, he inquired about their ownership.

"They belong to Lord Brok," the shepherds dutifully replied.

Meanwhile, the cat and Honza continued their journey, arriving at a picturesque valley where shepherds tended to magnificent herds of goats. These goats leaped and bounded with remarkable beauty and size, unmatched in the surrounding lands.

Curiosity piqued, the cat questioned the shepherds, "To whom do these splendid goats belong?"

"They belong to Lord Drak in the Yellow Mountain," the shepherds replied.

Once again, the cat issued its warning, and the shepherds, trembling in fear, promptly informed the king that these goats were indeed the possessions of Lord Brok.

As the king arrived at the valley and beheld the magnificent goats, he marveled at their unparalleled beauty. Eager to learn more about the enigmatic Lord Brok, he questioned the shepherds about their owner.

"They are the prized goats of Lord Brok," the shepherds affirmed.

The cat and Honza pressed on, venturing into a lush pasture where diligent cowherds tended to cows of extraordinary splendor. Each cow produced an abundance of milk, surpassing that of three ordinary cows combined.

Inquisitive as ever, the cat approached the cowherds, asking, "To whom do these magnificent cows belong?"

"They are owned by Lord Drak in the Yellow Mountain," the cowherds responded.

With a hiss and a firm warning, the cat compelled the cowherds to proclaim that these cows were the possessions of Lord Brok.

As the king arrived and laid eyes upon the extraordinary cows, he was amazed by their beauty and the sheer abundance of their milk.

"Whose cows are these? I have never witnessed such splendor in my entire kingdom," the king inquired.

"They belong to Lord Brok," the cowherds declared.

Filled with curiosity and a touch of bewilderment, the king marveled at the wealth and grandeur of Lord Brok. Eager to see his purportedly more magnificent castle, the king implored the cat, "I yearn to behold Lord Brok's residence. Pray tell, can I visit his castle?"

The cat, maintaining its mystique, replied, "You shall have to wait, Your Majesty."

Perplexed by this response, the king questioned, "Wait? For what?"

The cat, with an air of intrigue, cryptically replied, "Patience, Your Majesty. The wait shall be worthwhile."

The king, now even more intrigued, resolved to bide his time. Meanwhile, the cat hurried back to Honza, urging him to walk ahead of the royal procession by at least an hour. Though reluctant, Honza yielded to the cat's guidance and walked ahead as instructed.

As the cat and Honza continued their journey, they encountered a vast expanse of green meadow, dotted with herds of horses, their coats gleaming in hues of gold and silver. Each horse possessed an indescribable beauty and immense value.

Inquisitive, the cat approached the horse herders, posing the question, "To whom do these magnificent horses belong?"

"They are the prized possessions of Lord Drak in the Yellow Mountain," the herders replied.

With a hiss and a menacing gaze, the cat demanded that the herders declare these horses as the property of Lord Brok, lest they suffer dire consequences.

As the king's procession arrived, the cat's influence lingered, compelling the herders to proclaim that these extraordinary horses belonged to Lord Brok.

Entranced by the resplendent horses before him, the king marveled, "Whose horses are these? They are unlike any I have ever seen!"

"They are the horses of Lord Brok," the herders declared.

The king, now consumed by curiosity and a burning desire to witness the unparalleled splendor of Lord Brok's castle, implored the cat, "I beseech you, lead me to Lord Brok's magnificent residence."

The cat, with a gleam of triumph in its eyes, responded, "Your patience shall be rewarded, Your Majesty. The time has come."

With Honza already positioned in front of the castle, the cat hurried back to join him. As the sun began to set, a thunderous rumble resonated through the air, causing the very ground to tremble. The castle shook as the dragon from the Yellow Mountain returned to its abode. Then, an eerie silence enveloped the surroundings.

In that moment, the entire castle seemed to come alive. Servants scurried about, bustling with activity, and Honza found himself at the threshold of a resplendent marble, gold, and silver castle that sparkled like a precious gem. Yet, an air of desolation still hung heavy in the atmosphere, as if the grandeur had long been forsaken.

Honza entered the castle, choosing a room to settle in, while the cat positioned itself at the entrance, a basket of wheat cakes in its paws. It patiently waited, knowing that the pivotal moment was drawing near. As midnight approached, thunder roared through the air, causing the earth to quake, and the entire castle trembled in response. The fearsome dragon from the Yellow Mountain emerged, its three colossal heads thrusting through the doorway.

"Let me in! Let me in!" the dragon roared, its voice reverberating through the halls.

"Just a moment, dear Mr. Dragon," the cat replied calmly. "Allow me to regale you with the extraordinary tale of the journey this wheat endured before it transformed into these delectable cakes."

The dragon, intrigued and momentarily distracted from its fury, listened intently. The cat began to narrate the arduous process, describing the toil and transformations the wheat underwent, weaving an intricate tale of harvest, threshing, milling, and more.

But as the dragon's patience wore thin, it bellowed once again, "Step aside and let me in!"

The cat, unfazed by the dragon's mounting anger, continued its narrative, savoring each drawn-out word. It described the wheat's journey through sieves, the sprinkling of flour, and the final culmination of its transformation into the very cakes it now held.

The dragon, now nearly bursting with frustration, bellowed once more, "Let me in!"

But the cat, with a sly smile, announced, "Behold! A beautiful and splendid maiden appears behind the rock!"

The dragon, its curiosity piqued, turned its three heads to catch a glimpse of the maiden. Yet, as its heads swiveled, the sun emerged from behind the rock, casting its radiant rays upon the dragon's scaly form. And in that instant, the dragon was transformed into stone, frozen in its place forever.

As the castle seemed to awaken from its slumber, bustling with life once more, Honza found himself the master of this newfound domain. The servants, previously frozen in time, now resumed their duties, serving him with utmost dedication. And within the castle's vaults, treasures beyond imagination awaited him—piles of gold, silver, and gemstones accumulated over centuries.

Amidst this grandeur, the cat approached Honza, its work completed. "My dear Honza, the time has come for me to bid you farewell," it said in a melodic voice.

Touched by a mix of gratitude and sadness, Honza replied, "You have brought me unimaginable fortune and happiness. How can I ever repay you?"

The cat transformed, its sleek fur replaced by the ethereal feathers of a white dove. It fluttered its wings gently, a serene smile adorning its beak. "You have already rewarded me, dear Honza, with your unwavering love and trust," it cooed. "I am now free, released from the enchantment that bound me. Remember our time together fondly, and may happiness forever be yours."

With that, the white dove soared into the sky, disappearing into the vast expanse above. Honza watched with a mixture of joy and nostalgia, forever grateful for the faithful companion who had guided him to a life of prosperity and fulfillment.

And so, as the days And so, as the days turned into weeks and the weeks into months, Honza embraced his role as the ruler of the land. With wisdom and compassion, he governed justly, bringing prosperity and joy to his people. The news of his remarkable journey and newfound wealth spread far and wide, captivating the hearts of neighboring kingdoms.

Upon the passing of the old king, Honza's virtuous rule and reputation reached the ears of the royal court. In his final moments, the king bequeathed his own land to Honza, recognizing him as a worthy successor to the throne.

And so, with the support of his subjects and the love of his people, Honza ascended to the throne, bringing an era of peace and prosperity to the realm. He married the youngest princess, uniting their kingdoms in harmony and forging strong alliances with neighboring lands.

The memory of the cat, now a cherished legend, lived on in the hearts of the people. Honza erected a statue in the castle courtyard, immortalizing the loyal feline companion who had paved the way for his triumph.

Years passed, and Honza's reign remained a golden age in the annals of history. His name echoed through the generations, a symbol of resilience, courage, and the power of friendship. The tale of Mr. Dragon in the Yellow Mountain became a beloved fairytale, inspiring children and adults alike to embrace kindness, loyalty, and the belief that even the humblest beginnings can lead to greatness.

And as for Honza, his heart was forever grateful to the cat that had transformed his life. He often found himself stroking the statue's cold marble, whispering words of gratitude into the wind, knowing that the spirit of the faithful feline had guided him on a journey beyond his wildest dreams.

And thus, the story of Mr. Dragon in the Yellow Mountain became etched in the tapestry of folklore, reminding generations to come that true wealth lies not in material possessions, but in the bonds we form and the love we share along life's winding path.

The Magic Ring

Once upon a time, three brothers embarked on a quest to seek their fortunes in the vast world. Their wise old mother bestowed upon each of them a generous sum of three hundred gold coins to set the foundation for their future endeavors.

The eldest brother, driven by commerce and ambition, invested his share in purchasing a shop, thereby transforming himself into a merchant. The middle brother, with dreams rooted in the soil, acquired a plot of land, determined to become a prosperous farmer. However, the youngest brother harbored a different plan. He resolved to venture far and wide, his heart set on bestowing a hundred gold coins upon the first person he encountered.

And so, he set forth on his odyssey and soon came across a weary traveler burdened with a bag slung across his back. Within the confines of that bag rested a small cat. Staying true to his word, the young man tendered a hundred gold coins to the stranger, who, in turn, entrusted him with the feline companion. Curious about this exchange, the old mother questioned her son, "What do you plan to do with that cat?" But the son, silent and resolute, departed the following day, declaring, "I shall give a hundred gold coins to the first person fate brings across my path!"

It wasn't long before destiny intervened, introducing him to a fellow wayfarer, who carried a dog tucked away in a satchel. Once again, the young man fulfilled his promise, exchanging a hundred gold coins for the canine companion. Returning home with the newfound pets, he faced his mother's reproachful gaze. "Why do you persist in acquiring these animals? What benefit shall they bring you?" she queried. Undeterred, the young man remained steadfast, and on the third day, he embarked anew, his resolve unshaken to give a hundred gold coins to the first person he encountered.

During his journey, a serendipitous encounter with a mystical being unfolded. The young man noticed a slender silver ring adorning the spirit's finger and promptly offered a hundred gold coins in exchange for it. As the transaction concluded, the spirit vanished from sight, leaving the young man bewildered yet hopeful.

Returning homeward, his thoughts consumed by the mysterious ring, he inadvertently turned it, and a resounding voice emanated from within, inquiring, "What is your deepest desire?"

Without hesitation, the young man declared, "I wish to wed a princess!"

"As you wish," responded the enigmatic voice within the ring.

With newfound determination, the young man, accompanied by his loyal cat and dog, presented himself before the reigning king. Bowing deeply, he humbly implored, "Would you honor me with the hand of your illustrious daughter in marriage?"

The king, intrigued yet cautious, responded, "Should you construct a castle surpassing the grandeur of my own, you shall earn the right to claim her."

Once more, the young man bowed, assuring the king that his words would come to fruition. He turned the enchanted ring, channeling his desire into reality, a castle more magnificent than the king's palace emerging with the break of dawn.

When the king beheld the splendor of the new edifice, he marveled, "Truly, his palace surpasses mine in sheer beauty!"

However, when the young man sought to claim his bride, the king hesitated, subjecting him to yet another test. "Should you build a glass bridge spanning the river, connecting our domains, then and only then shall my daughter be bestowed upon you," proclaimed the king.

Harnessing the power of the ring, the young man commanded the spirits to construct a mesmerizing glass bridge throughout the night. Bound by his word, the king had no choice but to honor his promise and grant the young man his daughter's hand in marriage.

Yet, unbeknownst to the young man, the princess held a clandestine affair with a lover residing in the distant ninth kingdom. During their first night together, while the young man slumbered, the princess cunningly seized the magic ring from his finger and fled with her lover to the realm of the ninth kingdom, where they united in matrimony.

When the young man awoke, he discovered the princess's absence and the loss of the precious ring. Determined to reclaim his beloved and the enchanted ring, he turned to his faithful companions, the cat and the dog, entrusting them with the task of locating the stolen treasure. Together, the resolute cat and dog embarked on an arduous journey across nine kingdoms, relentlessly scouring for any trace of the elusive ring.

After an arduous search, the valiant duo arrived at a humble abode, where three sorcerers congregated before an imposing chest. Eavesdropping from a nearby window, the cat and dog overheard their devious plot.

"We shall conceal the ring within this chest, alongside priceless gemstones, and sink it deep into the unfathomable depths of the sea, ensuring that no suitor shall ever lay hands upon it," one sorcerer schemed.

Seizing the opportune moment, the dog boldly knocked on the door. Startled, the sorcerers welcomed the unexpected visitors, gratefully accepting their offer of assistance. The dog set to work, tirelessly gathering firewood, while the cat diligently attended to the household chores, ensuring the sorcerers remained blissfully oblivious to their true intentions.

Observing the sorcerers' slumbering forms stretched across benches, the cunning cat concocted a plan. Searching for a mighty and robust mouse, she captured the creature, firmly holding it in her paw, and issued a warning, "Retrieve the ring concealed within this chest, or face my wrath and unyielding claws!"

The mouse, obedient yet burdened by discomfort, began gnawing at the chest's wooden exterior. Moments later, it cried out in agony, lamenting the pain inflicted upon its delicate teeth.

"Persist and continue gnawing!" the cat commanded, her eyes fixed with an unwavering gaze. "Should you falter, I shall make a meal of you!"

Compelled by fear, the mouse resumed its task, persistently gnawing a second hole, but its agony persisted, its cries resounding through the room.

"Endure the pain and carve a third hole!" the cat urged, her voice laced with authority. And so, the determined mouse obeyed, gnawing through the final barrier, retrieving the elusive ring, and placing it within the cat's awaiting paw. In a swift motion, the cat swatted the mouse, reproaching it, "Why did you not hasten your efforts?"

With the ring in their possession, the cat and the dog swiftly departed, determined to reunite their master with his lost love. However, fate dealt a cruel blow when the cat, exhausted from the arduous journey, engaged in a heated argument with the dog.

Indignant, the cat reproached the dog, exclaiming, "I retrieved the ring, yet you refuse to carry me across the seas!" Unbeknownst to the feline, her words dislodged the ring from her mouth, causing it to plummet into the depths of the ocean. Determined to rectify their misfortune, they reached an island and cast their nets into the sea, hoping to reclaim the ring from its watery grave. The persistent grip of hunger gnawed at their stomachs, compelling them to embark on a quest to ensnare and procure fish for sustenance. Amidst their catch, a stroke of fortune smiled upon them as the dog discovered the lost ring nestled within the mouth of a fish. Rejoicing at their triumph, they rested, replenishing their strength before embarking on the final leg of their mission.

With the ring once again in their possession, the unwavering trio returned to their master. The young man, filled with renewed hope, invoked the ring's mystical powers, summoning his beloved wife from the distant ninth kingdom. Miraculously, she materialized before him, her eyes brimming with astonishment and remorse.

United once more, the young man, his wife, and their faithful companions embarked on a continued journey, traversing vast landscapes until they reached a tranquil field. While the young man's trust in his wife remained steadfast, his intuitive pets sensed an undercurrent of deceit.

In the field, they encountered a trio of thieves embroiled in a heated dispute over their ill-gotten gains—a cloak enabling flight, a pair of shoes returning one to the ground, and a samovar with twelve spouts, each dispensing a distinct hot beverage.

Intrigued by the commotion, the young man intervened, offering a resolution to their strife. Crafting a blowpipe from a slender reed, fashioning arrows with deftness, he proposed a competition. "Whosoever retrieves the arrow I shall shoot into yonder fence shall claim the entirety of the stolen treasures."

His words ignited a frenzied race as the thieves dashed towards the distant target. Meanwhile, seizing the opportunity, the young man donned the magical shoes, enveloped himself in the cloak's ethereal embrace, and cradled the samovar, soaring skyward and leaving the thieves bewildered and empty-handed upon their return.

Guided by his instincts, the young man winged his way to a rocky outcrop amidst the sea, where his wife sat alone, her heart teeming with guilt. Seating himself beside her, they engaged in earnest conversation. In a tender moment, she implored him, "Rest your weary head upon my lap."

Yet, as he leaned towards her, the true depths of her treachery revealed itself. She callously pushed him off the rock, her intent veiled in the belief that he would meet his watery demise. However, the enchanted shoes safeguarded him, gently guiding him back to the safety of the shore. Undeterred, he soared back to the rocky perch, taking his loyal cat and dog with him, embracing them as steadfast allies.

With a newfound clarity, the young man relinquished his attachment to his unfaithful wife. Acknowledging her fickle desires, he uttered, "Why did she flee from me? Surely, she no longer yearns for my companionship. In truth, I require naught but the unwavering loyalty of my cherished cat and dog."

From that moment onward, the young man lived a life brimming with contentment, forever accompanied by his devoted animal companions. Their bond, unbreakable and pure, led him to a state of profound and lasting happiness, spanning the length of his days.

And thus, in a contemporary retelling of this timeless tale, we learn that loyalty and companionship surpass the allure of fleeting desires, guiding us toward true fulfillment and enduring joy.

Skřítek The Little Gnome

Have you ever heard of gnomes? They are tiny beings, dwelling underground and within rocks, safeguarding precious ores and treasures. Sporting snug leather pants, blue jackets, red caps, and brown aprons, they dangle vibrant little lamps from their belts to illuminate their way through the dark underground tunnels.

In the mountains, lived the destitute weaver, Josífek, trudging along a forest path toward his humble abode. He shared a small, solitary wooden cottage with his wife. Both toiled ceaselessly, from dawn till dusk, and sometimes late into the night. His wife would spin yarn on the spinning wheel, while Josífek sat at the loom, diligently weaving. However, despite their tireless efforts, they struggled to make ends meet. People paid scanty sums for their wares, and during times of meager harvests, they suffered immensely during the harsh winter months. Occasionally, heavy rains would pour, causing the nearby stream to flood, inundating their dwelling and rendering work impossible for several days.

Yet, Josífek and his wife remained content, harboring no complaints about their fate. They lived with deep reverence for God and their circumstances. They couldn't relocate from their cottage due to financial constraints, and as they were advanced in years, they preferred not to seek refuge in a stranger's place or live on rent.

Thus, they exhibited patience and embraced their lot with resignation.

This time, in spring, the flooding engulfed their entire cottage. Josífek, undeterred, decided to journey to the nearby town to sell their goods and acquire essential food supplies. As he ascended the hill, he pondered if the waters would recede by the time he returned home. While traversing the woods, he suddenly heard moans and sighs emanating from the dense thicket of ferns.

Josífek halted, attentively tuning in to the sounds. The moaning ceased momentarily, only to resurface again.

"Perhaps there is a lost child in need!" Josífek pondered. He veered off the path, making his way toward the dense thicket, pausing intermittently to listen. As he neared the ferns, rustling ensued, accompanied by suppressed moans.

Josífek reached the spot and, parting the ferns, discovered a little gnome lying on the ground. A large stone had pinned his leg, immobilizing him. The gnome wriggled and struggled, attempting to free himself, fearing the approaching human. However, Josífek hurried to his aid, soothing him with reassuring words, "Fear not, fear not. Wait, I shall set you free!" The gnome stared at him intently, remaining motionless as Josífek leaned against the boulder. Despite its weight, Josífek managed to lift it sufficiently for the gnome to extract his leg.

"For this deed, I shall reward you!" exclaimed the gnome in a delicate voice, stomping his foot, and instantaneously disappearing into the ground.

Josífek crossed himself, shaking his head at the extraordinary encounter, and continued on his path. He reached the small town, successfully sold his merchandise, and procured essential provisions before embarking on the journey back home.

By the time he arrived, the water had subsided, allowing their cottage to dry out. The following day, Josífek and his wife resumed their work, grateful that the calamity hadn't inflicted significant damage upon them. As night fell, they retired, offering gratitude that their misfortunes hadn't escalated. However, during the night, they were abruptly awakened by a commotion. Moonlight streamed through the window, illuminating their living room, which was now teeming with bustling figures. Tiny gnomes hopped and scurried around the loom, filling the room with their energetic presence. Familiar weaving noises resonated in the air, and Josífek's gaze settled upon a gnome seated at the loom, while others scuttled about. One gnome occupied the spinning wheel, and four others operated it with precision. Muffled murmurs and various sounds, like the tapping of hammers and soft footsteps, emanated from outside.

Initially startled, Josífek and his wife found solace in crossing themselves and succumbed to a deep slumber, as if enchanted. Meanwhile, the gnomes continued their industrious work in the living room. When Josífek and his wife awoke the next morning, they surveyed their surroundings with astonishment. They remembered the nocturnal revelry and ethereal visitation, initially dismissing it as a dream. But behold! Towering stacks of exquisitely woven fabric and bountiful yarn adorned the loom, astounding the weaver and his wife. Their eyes widened in disbelief. Upon careful assessment, they realized that the goods were worth a substantial fortune in gold. Moreover, Josífek's wife discovered three minuscule golden nuggets, resembling hazelnuts, meticulously placed upon the table.

"Undoubtedly, this is the work of the gnome I rescued in the forest!" Josífek proclaimed, silently expressing heartfelt gratitude to the benevolent forest dweller for his extraordinary assistance. However, as Josífek stepped outside the cottage, his amazement only grew. Overnight, the gnomes had erected a robust stone embankment behind their dwelling, shielding it from the fiercest floods. From that day forward, on the anniversary of Josífek's benevolent act toward the distressed gnome, the mountain spirits paid him regular visits, weaving and spinning remarkable goods just as they had before. They consistently left behind three nuggets of gold, each the size of a hazelnut, as tokens of their appreciation.

Thus, poverty and hardship were banished from the humble cottage. Josífek and his wife continued to lead a modest and reverent life, offering silent gratitude in their hearts to the kind gnome who had forever changed their fortunes.

Little Tom Thumb

Once upon a time, a king was strolling in his carriage when he spotted a small cottage near a field. The cottager was diligently plowing the field with one horse, but to the king's surprise, there was another horse nearby plowing on its own. Intrigued, the king ordered a halt to observe this peculiar sight and struck up a conversation with the cottager.

"Who is plowing with the other horse?" the king inquired.

"That would be my eldest son," replied the cottager.

Curiosity piqued, the king asked, "Would you consider selling your son?"

"God forbid! How could I ever sell my own flesh and blood?" the cottager exclaimed, appalled at the suggestion.

"Then sell me instead, father!" shouted Tom Thumb, who was hidden amidst the mounds of earth. He was so minuscule that he remained unseen.

Thus, the father agreed and sold Tom Thumb to the king, who promptly placed him in his pocket. However, unbeknownst to the king, his pocket also contained his precious gold coins. Tom Thumb, with his keen eyes, noticed the glimmering coins and immediately called out to his father, proclaiming:

"Father, come with me! Accompany me!"

Obediently, the father followed, and Tom Thumb began discreetly discarding the king's gold coins, one by one, from the royal pocket until they adorned the ground. When he finished, Tom Thumb declared:

"Father, father, you may now return!"

And so, the father retraced his steps, diligently collecting each coin along the way.

Subsequently, they reached the grand castle, where the king instructed Tom Thumb, saying:

"Remove my shoes and stockings, and dry them for me!"

Tom Thumb dutifully unlaced the king's shoes and placed them inside the oven. As for the stockings, he hung them over a water pitcher to dry.

The next morning, the king impatiently demanded, "Fetch my stockings and shoes!" Tom Thumb presented the stockings first, but they were so saturated with water that a puddle formed beneath them. Frustrated, the king bellowed, "Now bring me my shoes!"

Tom Thumb complied, but instead of presenting intact shoes, he only provided a fragment of one sole and a solitary heel from the other. Handing them to the king, he cheekily remarked, "They are perfectly dry!"

"Incredibly dry, indeed! For this insolence, you shall receive a thrashing!" the king retorted, attempting to seize Tom Thumb. However, the cunning little fellow swiftly eluded capture, scurrying to his bed and burying himself within the straw. The king and his attendants searched high and low, but Tom Thumb concealed himself so skillfully, like a tiny mouse, that he remained undiscovered.

Ultimately, the straw from the bed was removed and fed to the ox, who unsuspectingly consumed the straw along with Tom Thumb.

The following morning, as the maidservants entered the courtyard, they were startled to hear a voice emanating from within the bull's belly:

"Good morning! Good morning!"

Initially taken aback, the maidservants quickly informed others, leading to the bull's eventual slaughter. However, despite their thorough search, Tom Thumb remained elusive within the bull's stomach and intestines. Thus, these organs were transported to the field, where a pack of wolves arrived. One ravenous wolf devoured the stomach, unwittingly ingesting Tom Thumb as well.

Later that night, the hungry wolf approached a nearby sheepfold, intent on capturing a sheep.

Yet, from within his belly, Tom Thumb called out:

"Shepherd, shepherd, the wolf wants to devour your flock!"

Startled by the unexpected warning, the shepherd swiftly awoke and began shouting, causing the frightened wolf to retreat empty-handed. This scenario repeated over several nights, leaving the wolf famished and frustrated. Realizing that Tom Thumb was consistently foiling his plans, the wolf finally spoke up:

"Listen, this arrangement isn't working out for either of us. I'm starving, and you're stuck inside my belly. I propose we strike a deal."

Intrigued, Tom Thumb replied, "Go on, what is your proposition?"

The wolf explained, "I will release you from my belly, but in return, you must help me find sustenance."

Agreeing to the wolf's terms, Tom Thumb said, "Very well, I will leave your belly.

However, you must carry me all the way to my father's house."

The wolf nodded, and with Tom Thumb nestled safely within, they raced towards the cottage. Upon reaching their destination, Tom Thumb made a request, "Carry me to the hallway, just outside the door."

The obliging wolf carried him to the hallway as requested. But as soon as they arrived, Tom Thumb began shouting, "Father, father, there's a wolf in the hallway!"

Startled by the commotion, Tom Thumb's father rushed to the scene, armed with a weapon. With one swift strike, he swiftly vanquished the wolf, freeing his beloved son from its belly. In gratitude, they fashioned a beautiful bag from the wolf's skin, carefully placing the royal coins inside it for safekeeping.

From that day forward, Tom Thumb and his father lived comfortably, no longer burdened by poverty or hardship. They cherished the bag made from the wolf's skin as a reminder of their extraordinary journey and the cleverness that had brought them fortune. And so, they lived happily, with the memory of their remarkable adventure etched in their hearts.

Werewolf

Once upon a time, in a magnificent kingdom, there reigned a wise and noble king. His dominion was vast, and his heart overflowed with love for his beloved queen and their precious daughter, a radiant little princess. The child was the epitome of beauty and grace, cherished by her parents above all else. Alas, fate is a capricious force, for tragedy struck when the queen fell gravely ill and succumbed to her ailment. The entire realm mourned the loss of their beloved queen, and the king, consumed by grief, swore to never marry again, finding solace solely in the presence of his dear daughter.

Years passed, and the princess blossomed into a stunning young lady, showered with endless affluence and indulgence by her doting father. She was attended to by numerous maids and ladies-in-waiting, among whom was a widow with two daughters. This woman was adept at weaving webs of deceit, disguising her malice with honeyed words and an alluring façade. Beneath her silk-smooth exterior, however, dwelled envy and treachery. As soon as the queen had departed this world, the wicked widow concocted a sinister plan to ascend the throne herself, with her daughters by her side. She began ingratiating herself with the young princess, employing flattery as her weapon of choice. Yet, beneath the veil of her praises, her words subtly insinuated that the princess would only find true happiness if the king were to seek a new wife. Naïve and trusting, the princess, like all children, accepted the woman's words as genuine and began to believe them herself.

One day, the princess inquired of the widow which woman would make a suitable queen for her father. The cunning woman responded, her voice dripping with honeyed sweetness, "It is not my place to offer advice in such matters. However, I can say this much: let the king choose a queen who will cherish you. And if fate were to smile upon me and the king were to select me, I would ensure your well-being. If you wished to cleanse your hands, my daughters would hold the basin for you, and the other would present you with a towel."

Thus spoke the artful schemer, and the princess, trusting as all children are, believed her with unwavering sincerity. From that moment forth, the princess found no peace until her heartfelt desire for a benevolent lady-in-waiting to become her stepmother was granted. The king, torn by hesitation, yielded to the princess's persistent pleas, although it went against his own wishes. He agreed, on one condition: that if the princess ever grew unhappy with her stepmother or stepsisters, she would not voice her complaints. Joyfully, the princess pledged her unwavering allegiance to her father's condition, sealing the agreement that the king would marry the lady-in-waiting and elevate her to the position of queen.

Several years elapsed, and the princess, unparalleled in her beauty, captivated all who beheld her. On the other hand, the queen's daughters, wretched and malicious, garnered no affection from anyone. Princes from far and wide journeyed to court the princess, vying for her favor, while the queen's daughters were shunned by suitors, their existence mere afterthoughts. This stoked the flames of resentment within the wicked stepmother's heart, who had yearned for one of her daughters to win the prince's affection. Determined to thwart the impending nuptials, she set forth to sabotage the young couple's union, her mind consumed by thoughts of their separation.

Opportunity presented itself when news arrived of an enemy invasion, compelling the king to embark on a war. It was then that the true nature of the stepmother was revealed. With the king's departure, she shed her mask of kindness and unleashed her cruelty upon the princess, subjecting her to harsh treatment and unrelenting torment. The stepmother berated and struck the princess daily, while her daughters followed suit, mirroring their mother's wickedness. But their malevolence was not reserved solely for the princess; they directed their cruelty towards the prince as well.

One fateful day, as the prince ventured into the forest for a hunting expedition, the wicked queen seized the opportunity to unleash her dark magic upon him. With a vile incantation, she cursed him, transforming him into a fearsome werewolf, doomed to roam the wilderness until death. When news of the prince's disappearance reached the princess, her heart was overcome with sorrow. Day and night, she wept inconsolably, finding no solace in her stepmother's laughter, for the queen reveled in the success of her wicked plan.

One day, while the princess sat alone in her chamber, she resolved to venture into the very forest where her beloved prince had vanished. Seeking respite from her sorrow beneath the open sky, she beseeched her stepmother for permission to take a walk. Reluctantly, the queen consented but commanded one of her daughters to accompany the princess on her journey. And so, the two girls set forth, with the princess wandering through the forest, her thoughts consumed by the prince, while her stepsister's resentment grew with every passing moment.

As they strolled through the woods, they stumbled upon a humble cottage nestled deep within the shadows. The princess, overcome by thirst, expressed her desire to enter and fetch a sip of water. Yet her stepsister, seething with anger, retorted, "Do you expect me, a noble princess, to enter such a hovel? If you wish to go, you can do so alone."

Unfazed by her stepsister's bitterness, the princess entered the cottage, where she discovered an elderly woman, her frail frame trembling with age. With her customary kindness, the princess greeted the old woman, saying, "Good evening, grandmother! Might I trouble you for a sip of water?"

The old woman, her voice filled with wisdom, replied, "Of course, my child. But do tell me, who are you, venturing into my humble abode with such warmth?"

The princess revealed her royal lineage and shared the weight of her sorrow, explaining how she had lost her beloved betrothed and feared she would never see him again. Tears streamed down her face as she poured out her heart, evoking a profound sense of empathy in anyone who listened. When she finished, the old woman spoke, her voice tinged with a hint of hope, "It is fortunate that you have confided in me, for I possess great wisdom. Listen carefully, for I may be able to guide you on your path. When you depart this place, you shall encounter a gladiolus unlike any other. It possesses extraordinary properties. Pluck it swiftly, and you shall receive further guidance."

Grateful for the old woman's counsel, the princess bid her farewell and departed the cottage, where her stepsister impatiently awaited her. Her stepsister scolded her bitterly, but the princess paid no mind, her thoughts consumed by the extraordinary gladiolus mentioned by the old woman. They continued their journey through the forest, and soon enough, the princess caught sight of a resplendent purple gladiolus sprouting from the ground. Overwhelmed with joy, she rushed towards it, only to find the flower vanishing and reappearing a short distance away. Driven by eagerness, the princess disregarded her stepsister's calls and pursued the elusive gladiolus. Time and again, the flower danced just out of her reach, growing more magnificent with each reappearance.

Unaware of her stepsister's frustration, the princess pressed on, her determination unyielding. Finally, the gladiolus led her to the base of a towering mountain. Looking up, she spotted the flower perched upon a bare rock at its summit, gleaming like a radiant star.

Without hesitation, fueled by her longing, the princess embarked on the arduous ascent, undeterred by the pain of scraped legs and prickling thorns.

After what felt like an eternity, she reached the mountaintop, where the gladiolus remained steadfast. With trembling hands, she plucked the flower, her heart brimming with joy and forgetfulness of the world below.

Yet, as she reveled in her triumph, a realization struck her: What would her stepmother say about her prolonged absence? Surveying her surroundings, she realized that the sun had already set, casting the forest into an impenetrable darkness. Fear gripped her, the prospect of spending the night on the mountain daunting. She settled upon a rocky outcrop, tears streaming down her face, as she pondered the wrath and reproach awaiting her return.

Under the veil of night, she heard a gentle voice, cutting through her despair, "Good evening, beautiful princess! Why do you sit here all alone, consumed by sadness?"

Startled, she turned to find a small, ethereal child standing before her—a being so pure and radiant that she had never beheld anything like it before. The child's hair shimmered like spun gold, and in their hand, they held a delicate ivory wand topped with a golden six-pointed star. Their smile banished her fear, and she spoke, her voice filled with trust, "I mourn, for I have lost my betrothed, and my heart knows no joy. Furthermore, I am lost in this forest, haunted by the fear of wild beasts."

"Oh, fear not," the child reassured her, their voice tender. "If you listen and follow my guidance, I shall aid you on your journey."

The child reached into their robes, retrieving a tinderbox, and continued, "Beautiful princess, let us first kindle a fire."

The princess nodded in agreement, and together they gathered dry leaves and twigs. As the flames danced upon the mountaintop, the child spoke once more, "Now, follow this path and seek out a cauldron filled with pitch. Retrieve it and bring it here."

The princess obeyed, her steps guided by the child's words. And when she returned, cauldron in hand, the child instructed her further, "Place the cauldron atop the fire."

With careful hands, she positioned the cauldron, and as the pitch within began to boil, the child's voice resonated, "And now, dear princess, cast your beautiful gladiolus into the seething pitch."

Reluctance tugged at her heart, for the flower held great significance to her. She hesitated, beseeching the child, "May I keep it, dear child? It is dear to my heart."

But the child responded with unwavering firmness, "Did you not promise to obey my every command? Trust in me and follow through, and you shall not regret it."

Resigned, she turned her gaze away, tears brimming, and bid farewell to the gladiolus. With a heavy heart, she tossed it into the boiling pitch, nearly overcome by grief.

In that very moment, a deep growl reverberated through the forest, as if a fearsome predator lurked in the shadows. The growl intensified, transforming into a bone-chilling howl that echoed through the mountains. The sound of snapping branches drew closer, and from the thickets emerged a colossal gray wolf, charging towards the mountaintop. Terror gripped the princess, her instincts urging her to flee, but the child's voice cut through her panic, "Quickly, jump down to the edge of the mountain with the cauldron. When the wolf passes, pour the pitch upon its head!"

With trembling hands, the princess clutched the cauldron and leaped to the precipice. As the wolf hurtled past her, she poured the scalding pitch upon its head, dousing it entirely. In an instant, a miraculous transformation occurred—the wolf's gray fur fell away, revealing a handsome young man standing before her. It was her beloved prince, freed from his cursed existence. Overwhelmed with joy, they embraced each other, laughter and tears mingling in their shared happiness. The prince expressed his deepest gratitude to the princess for her courage and to the child for their intervention.

Moments later, the three of them sat atop the mountaintop, engaging in warm conversation. The prince recounted his arduous journey as a cursed wolf, and the princess shared the torment inflicted upon her by her wicked stepmother and stepsisters. They basked in the tranquility of the night, their connection growing stronger with each passing moment. Unbeknownst to them, the stars began to fade, making way for the gentle hues of dawn.

As the first rays of sunlight broke over the horizon, illuminating the land below, the child's voice rang out once more, "Beautiful princess, apply this ointment to your eyes and behold the world anew."

The princess followed the child's instructions, rubbing the ointment over her eyes. When she opened them, she gasped in awe, exclaiming, "I see a rider on a spirited horse, galloping with great haste!"

The child smiled, their voice filled with affirmation, "It is a swift messenger sent by your father, the king. He and his entire army are en route, following closely behind."

The princess's heart swelled with hope and anticipation. However, the child advised her to wait a little longer, to observe what transpired. Time slipped by, the sun ascending higher in the sky, casting a warm glow upon the land.

Soon, the princess's gaze shifted towards the castle, and the child beckoned, "Turn around, beautiful princess. What do you see?"

She answered, her voice filled with curiosity, "I see people clad in mourning attire emerging from the royal palace. Some are heading towards the road, while others venture into the depths of the forest."

The child's voice resonated with knowing, "They are your stepmother's servants. Some are sent to welcome the king, while the rest embark on a futile search for you."

The princess's heart ached, her desire to go to her father growing stronger. Yet the child insisted on patience, urging her to wait a little longer. And so, they watched as time ebbed away, the sun's rays casting a radiant glow across the countryside.

At last, a small cloud appeared on the distant horizon, steadily growing larger as it approached. As it drew nearer, glimmers of light danced within it—helmets, weapons, and banners fluttering in the breeze. It was the royal banner. Overwhelmed with anticipation, the princess yearned to rush down and greet her father. But the child restrained her, advising her to wait once more.

And there, on the vast expanse before them, the child spoke, "Beautiful princess, turn around and look down at the castle. What do you see now?"

With a mix of excitement and trepidation, the princess shifted her gaze toward the castle below. She observed a flurry of activity as her father, the king, emerged, accompanied by her stepmother and stepsisters. The child prompted her, "Tell me, what unfolds before your eyes?"

"I see my stepmother and stepsisters, their faces hidden behind veils, clad in mourning attire," the princess replied. "They are feigning sorrow for my supposed demise. And my father... he stands before them, holding his sword and questioning their deceit."

The child nodded, their voice filled with certainty, "Your father desired to witness your presence no more, believing you to be lost forever. But the wicked facade of your stepmother has crumbled, and the truth has been revealed."

A surge of emotions coursed through the princess as she witnessed the unfolding scene. She yearned to rush down and comfort her grieving father, to assure him of her safety. But the child once again implored her to wait, to observe what would come next.

Time flowed on, the sun reaching its zenith, casting a golden glow upon the land. And then, from the horizon, a distant figure caught the princess's attention. Straining her eyes, she spoke with anticipation, "I see a multitude of people emerging from the castle. They are carrying a black coffin. My father... he has ordered it to be opened, and the queen and her daughters kneel before him, trembling."

The child's voice resonated with an air of triumph, "Your father demanded proof of their deceit, and now they are exposed."

Tears welled up in the princess's eyes, torn between the desire to rush to her father's side and the child's guidance to remain patient. And so, they waited, the sun's warmth enveloping them, as the events unfolded below.

Finally, the child beckoned, "Beautiful princess, turn your gaze to the distance. What do you see now?"

As the princess redirected her attention, her heart swelled with awe and disbelief. She exclaimed, her voice filled with wonder, "I see a grand procession on the horizon! Banners fluttering, soldiers marching, and my father at the forefront. They approach with great speed!"

The child smiled, their voice resonating with satisfaction, "That is your father, accompanied by his loyal subjects. Now, descend and bring joy to his grieving heart."

With renewed hope and anticipation, the princess, hand in hand with her prince, descended from the mountaintop. As they reached the king and his entourage, a wave of relief washed over him, his eyes wide with disbelief and overwhelming joy. Father and daughter embraced, tears streaming down their faces, while the prince, once cursed, was welcomed with open arms.

Amidst tears of happiness, the princess recounted the treachery of her stepmother, the sorcery that befell her prince, and the assistance of the mysterious child. Yet, when they turned to express their gratitude, the child had vanished, leaving behind only a sense of profound gratitude and the promise of eternal protection.

Together, the reunited family and their loyal subjects returned to the castle, where a grand celebration was held. The princess and the prince, their bond stronger than ever, departed for his kingdom, where they ruled with wisdom, compassion, and a deep appreciation for the happiness they had found.

And so, the story of the werewolf, with its trials and triumphs, served as a reminder that love, courage, and unwavering trust can overcome even the darkest of enchantments, leading to a happily ever after that would be cherished for generations to come.

The Elf and the Cook

Once upon a time in a majestic castle, an elderly count hosted esteemed guests and commanded his cook to prepare a colossal pot of delectable soup. The cook diligently placed the pot over the crackling fire, submerging tender chunks of lamb and beef, allowing the tantalizing aroma of the savory concoction to permeate the corridors. With a ladle in hand, the cook sat attentively, occasionally stirring the simmering broth.

Out of the blue, a diminutive figure materialized from beneath the stove, sporting a scarlet cap atop his head, velvet breeches, a leather jacket, and a lengthy gray beard. The little man gracefully bowed to the cook and implored, "Dear friend, I beseech you, grant me a taste of that sumptuous soup! My hunger is insatiable, and sustenance eludes me at every turn!"

Regretfully, the cook responded, "I'm afraid that's impossible. The soup is intended for our distinguished guests."

"Please, a mere morsel of the soup!" the little man pleaded once more.

"Very well," the cook relented, surrendering a ladle brimming with the savory liquid.

However, as soon as the elf clasped the ladle, he voraciously devoured the entire pot of soup with astonishing swiftness, leaving not a trace, before swiftly vanishing beneath the stove.

The cook was overcome with terror, unsure of his next move. Reluctantly, he resolved to approach his master and reveal the truth about the baffling incident. The cook lamented and offered sincere apologies, but initially, the count remained skeptical, dismissing the cook's account as mere fabrication. Yet, the cook persisted until the count finally acquiesced, calming his ire, and commanded the cook to procure more meat and prepare a fresh batch of soup. However, as a precaution, the count issued a stern instruction:

"Should that little man reappear, strike him on the head with the ladle!"

The cook departed and resumed his work, and ere long, a fresh pot of soup was gently simmering over the fire. As the savory aroma wafted through the air, the elf reemerged from his hiding place beneath the stove, casting an entreating gaze upon the cook, beseeching for a ladleful of soup to be poured into a tin container hanging from his neck.

"I'm afraid I cannot oblige," replied the cook with a hint of regret. "You exhausted the entire pot before, and the count has instructed me to strike you on the head should you return."

"Pray, spare me the blow, dear friend!" the little man implored. "Should you ever find yourself in dire straits, I shall come to your aid, rendering any assistance you may require. I have an ailing wife at home, and with her passing, I am left to fend for myself, bereft of nourishment and domestic support. I implore you earnestly, grant me half a ladle of soup, so my feeble child may find solace in its sustenance!"

Touched by the plight of the elf and his frail offspring, the cook's heart softened. He pondered, "Perhaps he will not exhibit the same voracity as before, and surely, a sick child requires but a meager portion." Succumbing to his empathy, the cook relented, stating, "Very well, take it!"

In an instant, the entire contents of the pot, including the succulent meat, vanished into the little man's container, leaving the pot barren. The elf promptly vanished, leaving the cook filled with trepidation, unsure of his next course of action. Resigned to his fate, the cook recognized that he had no choice but to rush to the count and confess the misfortune that had befallen him. With a heavy heart, he presented himself before his master, lamenting his actions and recounting the incident in earnest detail. The count's initial fury subsided only after the cook's unwavering insistence on the truth. Finally, the count regained composure and commanded the cook to chop fresh meat and prepare yet another batch of soup. However, he issued a stern warning:

"Should that little man dare to reappear, strike him down without hesitation! But make sure the soup is promptly readied!"

With a heavy burden upon his shoulders, the cook returned to his duties. The flames beneath the pot were rekindled, and the savory soup once again danced within the simmering vessel. As the fragrant aroma filled the air, a flicker of light emanated from beneath the stove, heralding the arrival of the mischievous elf. The cook, now cautious and resolute, seized the ladle firmly and confronted the intruder.

"You wretched scoundrel!" the cook exclaimed, brandishing the ladle. "Are you not aware that my master has commanded me to strike you down on sight?"

The elf pleaded desperately, his voice tinged with vulnerability. "I implore you, dear friend, consider the possibility that one day you may find yourself in dire need or suffering from hunger. In such a time, I shall come to your aid, offering my assistance wholeheartedly. My beloved child lies sickly, and my wife, now departed, can no longer provide sustenance or comfort. I beg of you earnestly, grant me at least half a ladle of soup, that my ailing child may find solace in its nourishment!"

The cook's heart softened as he contemplated the plight of the little man and his ailing child. Empathy welled within him, and he realized that compassion should triumph over vengeance. "Very well," the cook relented, his voice filled with compassion. "Take what you need."

In the blink of an eye, the pot was emptied once more, and the elf vanished, leaving the cook with a sense of trepidation and uncertainty. As expected, the cook yearned for recompense, hoping for a reward or token of gratitude. With trembling hands, he approached the count, recounting the incident, his voice quivering with anxiety.

"The little man returned for the third time, pilfering all the soup from the pot!" the cook declared.

Enraged beyond measure, the count exploded in a fit of anger. "You treacherous scoundrel!" he roared, his voice reverberating through the chamber. "However, due to your long and faithful service, I shall grant you one final night in my residence. Come morning, gather your belongings and depart with five plums as your sole provision!"

With a heavy heart, the cook bid farewell to the kitchen, contemplating his impending departure from the castle. Little did he know that the magical encounter he had experienced would lead him on a path of wonder and astonishment. As he ventured through the familiar chambers one last time, the ethereal figure of the elf appeared before him, his head wrapped in a bandage. He spoke gently, extending a gesture of farewell.

"Come, my dear friend, bid me farewell as well, for I have a token of appreciation to bestow upon you."

Curiosity piqued, the cook followed the little man's lead, venturing through a secret door that materialized beneath the stove. A hidden passage led them into a magnificent underground realm, adorned with opulent treasures, glistening gems, and treasures beyond imagination. The elf guided the cook through a series of rooms, each more enchanting than the last, until they arrived at a small chamber. In the center stood a table with numerous drawers, beckoning with an air of mystery. The elf opened one of the drawers and retrieved a small chest.

"Here, my dear friend, I have a gift for you," the elf said with a warm smile. "This is your reward for your kindness. Whenever you find yourself in need, simply tap your finger upon the lid of this chest and state your wish."

Overwhelmed with gratitude, the cook accepted the chest, awestruck by its magical potential. He thanked the elf profusely, feeling a deep sense of appreciation for the unexpected fortune bestowed upon him. With that, the elf accompanied the cook back up the stairs, bidding him farewell before vanishing alongside the concealed entrance to the underground realm. The cook stood in the kitchen, clutching the chest, half convinced that it had all been a vivid dream.

Suddenly, the head butler entered the kitchen, his gaze fixed upon the wondrous chest in the cook's possession. Consumed by curiosity, he couldn't contain his eagerness and implored the cook, "My dear friend, pray tell, whence did this magical chest come?"

The cook, overwhelmed with excitement, shared the extraordinary tale of his encounter with the elf and the subsequent reward bestowed upon him. Graciously, the cook bid the head butler farewell, as he was now compelled to embark on a new journey, armed with the remarkable power contained within the chest.

As he embarked on his travels, the cook found himself in need of various necessities. Remembering the elf's gift, he tapped his finger upon the chest and spoke his wishes. To his astonishment, each desire materialized before him. A sturdy bread bag appeared, accompanied by a warm coat, a trusty walking stick, a fashionable hat, comfortable shoes, and a myriad of other essential items. The head butler, witnessing this incredible spectacle, stood in awe, struggling to comprehend the enchantment that unfolded before his very eyes.

Intrigued and consumed by his desire for a similar chest of his own, the head butler resolved to mend his past misdeeds. Determined to earn the elf's favor, he hurriedly returned to the kitchen, rekindling the fire and setting the pot ablaze once more. Impatiently, he called out, "My dear friend, I beseech you, come and be my guest!"

In an instant, the elf materialized before him. "Why do you summon me?" the elf inquired, his voice tinged with suspicion. "I still have plenty of food from the cook."

The head butler, his heart brimming with avarice, extended an offering. "Taste this soup, dear elf, it is my gift to you."

The elf cautiously took a sip and, sensing the head butler's ulterior motives, spoke with a hint of warning. "Thank you kindly, but now I shall grant you a reward for your deeds."

Without expressing gratitude or humility, the head butler's sole intent was to acquire a chest of his own. As the elf led him to the underground realm and presented him with a similar chest, the head butler's true nature revealed itself. Lacking gratitude and respect, he harbored no genuine appreciation for the elf's generosity. Eager to return to the surface, he hastily bid the elf farewell.

As soon as the head butler stood before the count, pride and arrogance consumed him. "Look, Count, witness the wonders that occur when I tap my finger upon the lid of this chest!" he proclaimed, his voice brimming with conceit. He began tapping his finger upon the lid, filled with anticipation for the magical display that was about to unfold.

But to his dismay, instead of a joyous marvel, a malevolent force erupted from the chest. A vengeful little man with an iron club emerged, his eyes filled with fury and wrath. Swift as lightning, he pounced upon the count and the head butler, delivering relentless blows until they lay bruised and battered, their bodies crumpled in agony.

As swiftly as he had appeared, the vengeful elf disappeared, retreating back into the chest, which closed shut with an ominous creak. Silence engulfed the room as the count and the head butler lay half-dead upon the floor, their arrogance shattered by the consequences of their greed and disrespect.

Days turned into nights as the count and the head butler fought for their lives, nursing their wounds and pondering the folly of their actions. Their once-mighty spirits humbled, they understood the price they had paid for their lack of gratitude and the abuse of the elf's gifts.

Gradually, the count and the head butler regained their strength, their bodies healing but their souls forever marked by the scars of their transgressions. From that moment forward, they carried with them a profound appreciation for the kindness they had once scorned.

Meanwhile, the little elf, who had witnessed the true nature of the count and the head butler, decided to retreat from the human realm, never to be seen in the castle kitchen again. His kind heart wounded by their betrayal, he sought solace in the depths of the enchanted forest, where his magic would be cherished by those who truly deserved it.

As for the cook, he continued his journey, carrying the enchanted chest with him as a constant reminder of the power of compassion and gratitude. With each tap of his finger upon the lid, he utilized the chest's magic to assist those in need, offering kindness and support to strangers he encountered on his path.

And so, the story of the elf and the cook spread throughout the land, becoming a cautionary tale of the consequences of arrogance and greed, but also a testament to the transformative power of compassion and gratitude. The castle kitchen stood as a reminder of the mysterious encounters that could unfold when one's heart was open to the magic of the world.

As for the little elf, his presence lingered in the hearts of those who believed, serving as a whisper of enchantment and a reminder that kindness and appreciation were the truest forms of magic one could possess.

The Devil's Flute

Once upon a time, there lived a couple blessed with three sons. While the first two sons were known for their sharp wits, the youngest, Honza, was notorious for his utter foolishness. Behind their humble cottage, the family planted a patch of turnips, which soon became the target of a mischievous thief. Determined to protect their harvest, the brothers agreed to take turns guarding the turnips at night.

On the first night, the eldest brother concealed himself among the bushes behind the cottage. As the clock struck midnight, however, he succumbed to an irresistible drowsiness and fell into a deep slumber. At dawn, he awoke to find that the thief had once again ravaged the turnips, pilfering a significant portion. The following night, the second brother assumed the role of the guardian, but he too succumbed to the allure of sleep, leaving the thief free to snatch away more turnips.

Meanwhile, Honza lounged lazily atop the stove, resting his chin on his fists as he gazed outside, hunger gnawing at his belly. On the third day, he unexpectedly declared, "Shall I stand guard tonight?"

"Absurd, Honza! Such a responsibility is far beyond your grasp," his brothers scoffed.

Nevertheless, Honza insisted and prepared to take up the task of guarding. When darkness cloaked the land, he started to dance, swaying and twirling with fervor until the midnight hour arrived. He then lay down, but his keen eyes caught sight of a shadowy figure stealthily uprooting turnips. It was none other than the devil himself. Unfazed by fear, Honza confronted the devil, engaging him in a spirited wrestling match, dealing blows that elicited agonized yelps from his opponent. Curiosity piqued, Honza demanded, "Who are you?"

"I am the devil! And who might you be?" the devil retorted.

"By a twist of fate, I too am the devil!" Honza responded without hesitation.

"Very well, then let us journey together!" the devil proposed, and with the stolen turnips in their possession, they traversed hills and valleys.

Suddenly, Honza inquired, "What shall you offer me in exchange for these turnips?"

In response, the devil bestowed upon him a flute that harmonized melodies of various tunes when played. Satisfied, Honza accepted the gift, returned home, and ascended the stove, resuming his former posture.

"Where have you hidden the turnips, Honza?" his father bellowed. "They have all vanished!"

"I bartered them with the devil in exchange for this enchanting flute!" Honza revealed.

"Well, at least you obtained something!" his father conceded, and thus, the matter was laid to rest.

Located behind the cottage was a diminutive pigpen where three sows and their piglets dwelled. Honza, ever the eccentric, resolved to care for them. Doubting his abilities, his father questioned, "How do you intend to tend to them, foolish Honza? They will stray and be lost under your watch!"

Unyielding in his decision, Honza escorted the pigs to a verdant pasture. Soon, boredom crept upon him, and he retrieved the devil's flute, placing it to his lips. Instantaneously, the pigs and piglets commenced a lively dance, prancing and twirling in a whimsical display. Delighted by the spectacle, Honza continued playing the flute, and the animals merrily frolicked to the enchanting melodies.

Just then, the royal princess chanced upon the scene while traversing the nearby road. Mesmerized by the sight of the dancing pigs, she was captivated and immediately desired to possess such extraordinary creatures in the castle. With a determined stride, she approached Honza and requested to purchase one of the piglets.

Initially hesitant, Honza saw an opportunity for mischief and amusement. The princess, renowned for her beauty, always concealed her face beneath a thick veil, denying anyone the privilege of beholding her lovely countenance. Honza, mischievous as ever, grinned mischievously and said, "These piglets, my dear princess, are not for sale. However, if you are willing to unveil half of your face, specifically your mouth, I shall gift you one without charge."

Realizing that the piglets were beyond her reach unless she complied, the princess pushed back her veil, revealing the lower portion of her face. Honza's keen eyes discerned a small black dot adorning the left side of her mouth. With a playful smirk, he handed her the desired piglet. The princess, her prized possession secured, promptly departed for the castle in her ornate carriage.

Excitement rippled through the castle as the princess hastily sought an audience with the king, eager to share news of her miraculous acquisition. The entire court gathered, including the king and queen, who eagerly anticipated the grand spectacle of the dancing piglets. Alas, much to their dismay, the piglets merely scurried about, snorting and rooting their snouts into the ground, exhibiting no inclination to dance.

"Clearly, we require another piglet," the princess declared. "They shall find joy in each other's company, and then they shall dance!" Determined to acquire a companion for the piglets, she resolved to visit Honza once more on the morrow.

In the interim, Honza returned home with his two remaining piglets. His father, ever quick to anger, interrogated him without delay. "Where, pray tell, is the third piglet?"

"It has fled," Honza replied nonchalantly.

"Unyielding fool!" his father chastised, his temper flaring.

Undeterred by his father's reproach, Honza embarked on the following day's journey with his two loyal piglets and their sow. Once again, he employed the devil's flute, eliciting a joyous and animated dance from the swine. Observing from the lofty vantage point of the castle, the king and princess marveled at the spectacle. Eager to secure a second piglet, the princess dispatched her attendants to negotiate its acquisition. However, Honza, in his whimsical nature, insisted that the princess herself make the request.

Complying with Honza's peculiar demand, the princess arrived at his abode. Honza, with a playful glint in his eyes, declared that she must unveil her true face if she wished to secure the piglet. Aware that her beauty was a closely guarded secret, the princess hesitated. However, the allure of the piglet proved irresistible, and she unveiled her face, revealing eyes as blue as violets. Honza's gaze lingered, captivated by the mesmerizing hue, before ultimately relinquishing the second piglet to the delighted princess.

Returning to the castle with her newfound treasure, the princess once again anticipated a spectacle, eager to witness the piglets dance. Alas, her expectations were thwarted as the piglets remained stubbornly unresponsive, failing to exhibit even the slightest inclination for merriment.

"I conclude that a third piglet is necessary," the princess determined. "Undoubtedly, they yearn for the companionship of another, which shall coax forth their dancing spirits!" Resolute in her pursuit, she planned another visit to Honza's dwelling the following day, intent on acquiring the third and final piglet.

In the meantime, Honza returned home with the sow and a lone piglet, his father seething with anger at the perceived foolishness of his youngest son. Unperturbed by his father's ire, Honza maintained an air of indifference, climbing onto the stove and feigning slumber.

As the sun rose on the appointed morning, Honza embarked on his customary routine, leading the sow and piglet to the pasture. Before long, the princess arrived, her desire for the last piglet unwavering. Honza, feigning disinterest, attempted to deflect her request, but eventually, he relented, stipulating that she unveil her hair before receiving the coveted piglet.

The princess, prideful of her cascading tresses, hesitated at the thought of revealing her hidden beauty. However, consumed by her longing for the final piglet, she consented, revealing locks that shimmered with pure gold. Honza's gaze lingered upon the resplendent sight, marveling at the radiant strands. With a smile, he finally bestowed the princess with the third piglet, bidding her farewell as he returned home, accompanied solely by the sow.

Back at the castle, anticipation grew as the princess released the trio of piglets into the grand courtyard, the entire court assembled in eager anticipation. But, to their dismay, the piglets seemed indifferent to the grandeur of their surroundings, simply scampering about, their focus on rooting and snorting rather than dancing as expected.

Time passed, and the momentous occasion of the princess's nuptials drew near. The king, determined to find a worthy suitor, issued a proclamation throughout the realm, promising the hand of the princess, along with half the kingdom, to any who could decipher the markings upon her face, the hue of her eyes, and the shade of her hair. Suitors flocked from far and wide, each seeking to unlock the enigma that veiled the princess's beauty. Yet, one after another, they faltered in their attempts, unable to discern the secrets concealed beneath the princess's shroud.

Amidst the commotion and failed endeavors, Honza arrived at the castle, his brothers derisively mocking his audacity to compete for the hand of the princess. Ignoring their jeers, Honza stood tall, garbed in his finest attire, a newfound confidence emanating from within.

The king, amused by Honza's presence, greeted him with a laugh, while the princess, aware of the truth that lay behind the veil, suppressed a smile, her heart yearning for the one who had seen beyond her facade.

Undeterred by the skepticism surrounding him, Honza approached the king with unwavering determination. As the crowd hushed in anticipation, he spoke with eloquence and grace, his voice resonating with newfound wisdom. "Your Majesty, I come before you today not as the foolish boy you once knew, but as a transformed man. Allow me the chance to unravel the mystery that shrouds the princess, for I have gazed upon her true beauty."

Intrigued by Honza's bold claim, the king granted him an audience, while the court held their breath in anticipation. Stepping forward, Honza spoke with gentle reverence, recounting the details he had observed during his encounters with the princess. His words painted a vivid picture, unraveling the tapestry of her hidden features.

"The princess, fair and enchanting, possesses a small black dot on the left side of her mouth, a unique mark that sets her apart. Her eyes, a mesmerizing shade of blue akin to violets in bloom, captivate all who have the privilege to behold them."

As the words left Honza's lips, a gasp echoed through the court. The princess's veil quivered, a mixture of surprise and anticipation emanating from beneath. Honza had unveiled the secrets carefully guarded by the princess, exposing the truth that lay concealed. The courtiers exchanged glances, recognizing the accuracy of Honza's description.

With a hint of a smile playing upon her lips, the princess gracefully lifted her veil, revealing a visage adorned with the mark and eyes akin to a field of blooming violets. The court erupted in applause and whispers of admiration, for Honza had accomplished what no other suitor could—a feat that transcended the boundaries of perception.

Impressed by Honza's astuteness and captivated by his transformation, the king, a man of his word, fulfilled his promise. Honza, the once-foolish lad, now stood by the princess's side, his hand clasping hers in a pledge of eternal devotion. In due time, the king's demise led to Honza ascending the throne, uniting his wisdom, humility, and newfound kingly presence with the beauty and grace of his beloved princess.

As king and queen, Honza and the princess ruled the kingdom with fairness, compassion, and a touch of whimsy. They reigned over a land where wisdom and folly danced harmoniously, where the value of true perception was cherished, and where the transformative power of love was celebrated.

And so, the tale of Honza, the once-foolish lad turned wise and discerning ruler, became a legend passed down through generations—a testament to the power of insight, the allure of hidden beauty, and the everlasting magic found within the most unexpected of hearts.

Witches

Once upon a time, there lived a young lad named Václav. He was born into a humble family and felt the urge to explore the world and gain some life experience. One day, he arrived in a village where he learned that a farm was in need of a farmhand. Intrigued, he made his way to the farm, and the maid welcomed him with open arms. Václav was delighted to have found such a pleasant place, where work was plentiful, and there was always enough food to satisfy his hunger. Each day, he savored a plate of delectable pancakes or dumplings, relishing every bite. However, there was one peculiar mystery that puzzled him—the maid never seemed to prepare the dough, and there was no trace of sourdough anywhere in the house. Václav's curiosity was piqued, and he resolved to uncover the truth.

On the days when the maid was absent, a strict prohibition was enforced, preventing anyone from entering the room where Václav slept. The entire household was compelled to find repose in the annex or the attic. Intrigued by these peculiarities, Václav resolved to unravel the enigma that surrounded him. He said to himself, "There is a secret here, and I must unearth it!"

One evening, on the day the maid was scheduled to depart once again, Václav pretended to be fast asleep as he lay beneath the bench by the warm stove. The maid approached him and tried to rouse him from his slumber. "Václav, wake up and tend to the horses!" she called out. Despite hearing her words clearly, Václav snored loudly, refusing to stir. The maid prodded him and even pricked his feet with a needle, hoping to elicit a response. But Václav remained still as a stone. Frustrated by her failed attempts, the maid fetched a rake and reached beneath the chimney, where she concealed a pot of mysterious ointment. She anointed the rake with the potent substance, opened the window, perched herself upon the rake, and chanted, "Fly out, up and down, up and down, up!"

Observing the maid's actions intently, Václav seized the opportunity. He took another rake and smeared it with the same magical ointment. Settling onto the rake's wooden surface, he mimicked the maid's words, saying, "Fly out, up and down, up and down, up!" However, in his haste, he forgot to utter the crucial word "up" at the end. Consequently, when he launched himself out of the window, the rake carried him close to the ground instead of soaring high above the treetops. Václav found himself scraping against thorns and stones, enduring scratches and bruises. Nevertheless, he pressed on until he reached a solitary tavern nestled atop a hill. Exhausted yet determined, he crossed its threshold.

Inside the cavernous room, lively music reverberated, and Václav's eyes beheld a peculiar sight. Witches of every description reveled within, indulging in feasts, libations, and spirited dances. Over a hundred enchantresses filled the space, exuding an air of enchantment. To his surprise, Václav's maid spotted him amidst the revelry and hurriedly made her way toward him, casting an accusatory glance. "You devil! You feigned sleep when I attempted to awaken you, merely to sate your curiosity!" she exclaimed.

Despite her rebuke, the maid extended a jug of frothy beer to Václav, urging him to join in their ut promptly dismissed Václav from his duties, compensating him handsomely for his service, while issuing a stark reminder.

"Remember the oath you have taken! Speak of this to no one!" she admonished him.

Years passed, and Václav traversed various paths, toiling in numerous occupations. Eventually, he found love, settled into married life, and established a household of his own. Throughout his endeavors, he remained steadfast in his commitment to keep the secrets of the witches' hill locked away within his heart, refusing to divulge them to a single soul. Yet, one day, while tending to a docile cow near a babbling stream, Václav was overwhelmed by an irrepressible urge to unburden himself of the long-held secret. He sought solace beneath a hollow tree, pouring out his experiences and confessions to its venerable trunk. With a renewed sense of release, he herded the cow back home, finding solace in the weight lifted from his shoulders.

Several days later, a weary traveler sought respite beneath the very same tree. Drained from his journey, he succumbed to slumber beneath the tree's comforting shade. Unbeknownst to him, the ancient tree possessed a remarkable ability to retain the tales whispered in its presence. As the traveler slept, the tree shared the secrets it had absorbed from Václav's confessions, weaving the story into the traveler's dreams. Thus, at last, the long-guarded secret began to unfurl, no longer confined to the depths of Václav's conscience.

When the traveler awoke, he felt a peculiar sensation—an awakening of forgotten memories, as if a story had been whispered to him in his slumber. It was as if the very essence of Václav's secret had been entrusted to him. Overwhelmed by the weight of this newfound knowledge, the traveler contemplated the significance of the tale he had heard from the tree.

Driven by an unyielding desire to unravel the mystery further, the traveler embarked on a journey, traversing distant lands and seeking the counsel of wise sages and learned scholars. He shared with them the enchanting tale of

Václav and the witches, striving to decipher its hidden meanings and unravel the lessons concealed within.

The tale spread far and wide, captivating the hearts and minds of those who heard it. The secret of the witches' hill, once guarded so fiercely, was now an open secret, whispered from ear to ear. Its allure and mystique persisted, leaving an indelible mark on the tapestry of folklore.

And so, through the passage of time, the story of Václav and the witches became immortalized, transcending the boundaries of generations. It served as a cautionary tale, reminding humanity of the dangers of forbidden knowledge, the allure of curiosity, and the price one might pay for breaching the sacred pact of secrecy.

The Shepherd and the Princess

Once upon a time, in a distant land, there lived a humble shepherd who knew nothing beyond tending to his flock of sheep. He wore tattered clothes, with only one pair of undergarments and a coarse shirt to his name. However, destiny had grand plans for this simple shepherd.

On a serene Sunday morning, as the sun painted the sky with hues of gold, the shepherd herded his sheep closer to the church. A whispered curiosity tugged at his heart, compelling him to venture inside. Little did he know that a momentous announcement awaited him within those sacred walls. From the pulpit, the priest declared that the princess, the sole daughter of the king, had mysteriously vanished. The one who could find her would be granted her hand in marriage and bestowed with half of the kingdom.

A flame of determination ignited within the shepherd's soul. "I shall embark on this quest and find the princess!" he resolved with unwavering conviction.

Setting off on his arduous journey, the shepherd traversed through vast, dense forests shrouded in darkness. With each step, he pushed through the thick foliage until two grand castles loomed before him, a juxtaposition of beauty and grandeur. One castle stood majestic, larger than life, while the other possessed a subtle charm. Without hesitation, the shepherd chose the smaller castle, guided by an instinct that whispered of hidden secrets.

Within the castle's walls, silence reigned, save for the presence of an old maid who greeted him with curiosity. "How did you find your way here, little man?" she inquired.

The shepherd shared his tale, revealing his humble origins as a shepherd and his unyielding determination to find the princess.

The old maid pondered, her eyes filled with a mix of concern and caution. "The princess indeed resides here, but freeing her won't be an easy task," she warned.

Undeterred, the shepherd pleaded with the maid, his heartfelt sincerity piercing her defenses. Eventually, compassion softened her heart, and she extended her aid. Handing him a large bag filled with gleaming silver coins, she instructed him to hide it in the forest under the roots of an ancient oak tree. It must be concealed in a manner that he could retrieve it the following day. With gratitude in his eyes, the shepherd embarked on his appointed task, securing the bag of silver amidst the roots of the mighty oak.

Returning to the castle, the shepherd sought refuge alongside the old maid, patiently biding his time. Little did he know that the castle harbored a den of bandits. As night fell, the bandits arrived, their presence filling the air with an aura of danger. Their eyes fell upon the shepherd, curiosity burning in their gazes. They bombarded him with questions, seeking to unravel the mystery of his presence.

Guided by the old maid's wisdom, the shepherd skillfully responded, aligning his words with theirs. He proclaimed a desire to join their ranks, presenting himself as a kindred spirit in their illicit trade. Eager to welcome a fellow rogue, the bandits embraced him into their fold.

The next day arrived, a crucial test awaiting the shepherd. The bandits proposed a joint robbery, an ambush to plunder unsuspecting merchants. However, the shepherd, his mind shrewd and calculating, suggested an alternative approach. "Allow me to venture alone," he proposed. "Merchants are less fearful when confronted by an individual rather than a menacing gang."

Intrigued by his audacity, the bandits consented to his plan, setting off on their own criminal pursuits while the shepherd ventured deep into the forest. His steps led him to the old oak, where the hidden treasure awaited him. Retrieving the bag of silver, he triumphantly returned to the castle before the bandits arrived in the evening. Their eyes widened in disbelief as they beheld the riches he had acquired on his solo endeavor.

Impressed by the shepherd's prowess, the bandits hailed him as a skilled comrade. The leader of the gang, intrigued by the young man's abilities, expressed his desire to meet him in person. Unbeknownst to them, fate had woven a web of destiny, and the shepherd would soon seize his moment.

Meanwhile, the observant maid overheard their conversation. A mischievous smile danced upon her lips as she hatched a plan. "If you have such a remarkable companion," she suggested, her voice laced with cunning, "a celebration is in order. Send one of your comrades to the town to fetch wine, for he has brought forth a fortune and promises even greater riches!"

The bandits, enticed by the prospect of revelry, hastily prepared a carriage and instructed the shepherd to embark on the wine-fetching mission. Unbeknownst to them, the maid had slipped a note into his possession, secret instructions etched upon its surface. It detailed not only the procurement of wine but also the acquisition of a vial of sleeping potion.

Following the maid's guidance, the shepherd acquired the wine and discreetly obtained the sleeping potion, the elixir of dreams. Returning to the castle, he presented the wine to his unsuspecting comrades, blissfully unaware of the potion that awaited them within the goblets.

As night enveloped the castle, the bandits eagerly indulged in the wine, unknowingly sipping the potion-laced concoction. Gradually, weariness engulfed their bodies, and they succumbed to a deep slumber, motionless and oblivious to the world around them.

The moment the maid witnessed their sleep-laden state, she whispered to the shepherd, her voice brimming with urgency, "Now, take up your sword and sever the ties that bind them. Then proceed to the other castle."

Determined and resolute, the shepherd followed her instructions meticulously. Each bandit met their demise as his sword swung swiftly, severing the life that had once coursed through their veins. Once the grim task was complete, the shepherd cleansed himself, donning fresh attire that befit his newfound destiny.

Embarking upon the path to the leader's castle, the shepherd's heart pulsed with a mix of trepidation and anticipation. As he arrived, he was greeted with open arms, his deeds and the tales of his riches preceding him. The bandit leader, overflowing with gratitude, expressed his sincere appreciation for the bags of wealth the shepherd had brought forth.

Within the leader's chamber, the shepherd's gaze wandered and fell upon a majestic sword adorning the wall—a symbol of power and authority. His desire to wield such a weapon coursed through his veins, yet the strength to lift it eluded him. The bandit leader, sensing his longing, proposed a solution.

"I possess a vial of magic potion," he disclosed, retrieving a small phial from a hidden compartment. "Drink from this, and the strength to wield the sword shall be yours."

Eagerly, the shepherd accepted the vial and consumed its contents. A surge of power coursed through his being as he clasped the mighty sword, his grip firm and unwavering. With a triumphant flourish, he declared, "Now, the true treasures shall be mine!" In one swift motion, he beheaded the bandit leader, a final act of justice.

As the leader's head fell, a futile attempt to reunite with his body ensued, but the shepherd's resolute kick sent it spinning to the other side of the chamber, severing any hope of reunion.

Amidst the aftermath of the leader's demise, the shepherd's gaze fell upon a sight that stirred his heart—the princess, confined within an iron cage, her tears a testament to her captive plight. In that moment, their eyes locked, recognition and gratitude passing between them. Determined to free her from the clutches of captivity, the shepherd approached the cage, guided by the princess's whispered instructions.

With the aid of the keys she disclosed, the shepherd swiftly unlocked the iron cage, setting her free from her long and sorrowful confinement. Side by side, they made their way back to the old maid, their gratitude overflowing. In return for her assistance, the maid bestowed upon them a portion of their accumulated wealth, ensuring their prosperous journey.

With the princess by his side, the shepherd embarked on the path that would lead them back to her father's kingdom. Their journey wound through the depths of the dark forest until they reached a vibrant seaside town. Casting their gaze upon the vast expanse of the sea, uncertainty tinged their thoughts.

"Who knows what fortunes await us?" mused the princess, her voice laced with a mix of hope and apprehension. In a display of resourcefulness, she sewed a hidden pocket on the inside of the shepherd's coarse shirt. From her own possessions, she tore a silk scarf in half, presenting him with one piece. Alongside it, she bestowed upon him an earring, a ring from her finger, and half of a delicate chain that encircled her waist. With careful precision, she sewed the pocket shut, safeguarding their tokens of love and fortune.

Guided by the princess's wisdom, the shepherd arrived at an inn, their temporary sanctuary on the shores of the seaside town. Sensing their need for sustenance and security, the princess spoke with a purpose. "Craft a purse for our wealth, my love. Take it to the town and sell it, but demand no less than fifty thalers."

Committed to his role, the shepherd obediently fashioned a purse with skilled hands. Venturing into the town, he sought out a discerning buyer, negotiating with conviction until the purse exchanged hands, procuring the desired fifty thalers. Yet, temptation lurked, and the allure of a game of chance proved too much for the shepherd to resist. Enticed by the sight of wealthy gentlemen engrossed in a card game, he joined in, drawn by the prospect of increasing his fortune.

Fate, however, proved fickle, and the winds of luck shifted against the shepherd. Game after game, he found himself at the mercy of ill-fated hands until his entire fortune vanished. A cloud of desolation settled upon him as he made his way back to the princess, his heart heavy with regret.

Upon seeing his dejected countenance, the princess tenderly inquired, "Why do you carry such sadness, my love? Did you not receive the fifty thalers?"

A sigh escaped the shepherd's lips as he recounted his tale of waning luck. "Indeed, I received the sum," he confessed, "but my desire for fleeting riches led me astray, and I squandered it all."

Unyielding in her support, the princess remained steadfast, her love undiminished. Once more, she threaded her needle and sewed another purse, firm in her conviction that it held the key to their fortune. However, she impressed upon the shepherd a specific condition—he could only sell it to a ship captain, and he must demand no less than a hundred thalers.

Embracing her wisdom, the shepherd set forth to the bustling harbor, where destiny intertwined with opportunity. A discerning captain recognized the purse's worth and eagerly acquired it from the shepherd, parting with a hundred thalers in exchange. The transaction complete, the captain posed a question, curiosity gleaming in his eyes.

"Who crafted this exquisite purse?" he inquired, his gaze fixed upon the shepherd.

"My fiancée," the shepherd replied, a hint of pride gracing his voice.

The captain's interest piqued, he further inquired, "Where can I find her?"

"She awaits my return at a small inn within this very town," the shepherd responded.

Intrigued by the shepherd's tale, the captain extended an invitation. "Come back tomorrow, and bring your fiancée along," he instructed, a glimmer of excitement dancing in his eyes.

Following the captain's orders, the shepherd made his way back, eager to share the captain's invitation with the princess. As twilight cast its gentle embrace over the land, an unexpected sight caught the shepherd's attention. In the fading light, he witnessed a macabre scene unfolding within a nearby cemetery—two apparitions, once lifebound, now engaged in an ethereal dispute.

Drawing closer, the shepherd overheard their spectral quarrel. "You still owe me a hundred thalers!" one of them vehemently exclaimed.

Moved by their plight, the shepherd approached the restless souls, a compassionate light shining within his eyes. Without hesitation, he reached into his pockets, retrieving the very sum they sought. "Take this hundred thalers," he urged them, his voice resolute, "and may it bring you the peace you seek."

As the money exchanged hands, the two ethereal figures vanished, their debt finally absolved. Grateful, the shepherd continued his journey, arriving at the princess's side with a tale of redemption and compassionate deeds.

The next day dawned, marking their anticipated reunion with the captain. Guided by the princess's unwavering faith, the shepherd returned to the ship. To his astonishment, the vessel sailed alongside a magnificent ship, its grandeur unmatched. Excitement ignited within him as he stepped onto the deck, yet an eerie silence enveloped the air—the ship devoid of any living soul, despite its sails billowing with the wind's embrace.

Curiosity consumed the shepherd, leading him below deck. A feast awaited him, the table adorned with an array of tantalizing dishes. Hunger gnawing at his stomach, he succumbed to temptation, partaking in the sumptuous fare. Yet, as morsels met his lips, a disembodied voice called out from the deck, urging him to emerge.

Startled, the shepherd hastened to the deck, only to find emptiness surrounding him. Confusion clouded his mind as he descended once more, resuming his interrupted meal. The voice persisted, growing louder with each summons. Determined to uncover the source, the shepherd ascended to the deck once again, peering into the vast expanse before him.

Finally, at the bow of the ship, a figure lay motionless on the ground. Eagerly, the shepherd encouraged him to join the feast, unaware of the otherworldly presence before him. The figure, now revealed, spoke with solemn gratitude, revealing his identity.

"I am the dead man to whom you generously paid a hundred thalers in the cemetery," he disclosed, his voice carrying an ethereal timbre. "In gratitude for your kindness, I gift you this ship—a vessel sailing towards the city where the captain holds the princess captive. With this, you shall arrive before their ill-fated union. When the anchor lifts itself and flags adorn the masts, proclaim loudly, 'Load and fire!' And when a white flag emerges from the tower of the royal palace, declare, 'Cease fire!'"

In awe of the supernatural occurrence, the shepherd accepted the ship as his bestowed reward. Following the dead man's instructions, he set sail, guided by the currents of fate towards the city where the princess's destiny awaited. The ship glided through the harbor, the anchor lifting of its own accord, and colorful flags unfurled upon the masts.

Remembering the dead man's words, the shepherd's voice echoed across the waters, resounding with authority, "Load and fire!" As if possessed by a hidden force, the cannons roared to life, their thunderous blasts shaking the city's windows and reverberating through its walls. Chaos ensued as citizens sought shelter from the unexpected onslaught.

High above, atop the tower of the royal palace, a white flag ascended, its ethereal hue fluttering in the wind. Recognizing the signal, the shepherd commanded, "Cease fire!" And just like that, the cannons fell silent, the city engulfed in an eerie calm.

Word of the shepherd's arrival reached the king's ears, and he summoned him for an audience. Anticipation gripped the kingdom as the shepherd disembarked from his ship and made his way towards the regal palace. However, at the palace gates, the guards, judging him by his humble appearance, barred his path.

With determination burning within him, the shepherd returned to his ship, issuing a decisive command, "Load and fire!" The cannons roared once again, their echoes rattling the palace walls. The guards, taken aback by the sudden display of power, quickly relented, allowing the shepherd passage into the castle.

The princess, in her wisdom, entreated her father to join her in her chambers. With a heart filled with love and gratitude, she revealed the shepherd's heroic deeds, sharing the tokens of their love and fortune that he carried with him—a scarf, an earring, a ring, and a fragment of a delicate chain.

As realization dawned upon the king, his eyes brimmed with tears of joy and relief. Eager to meet the shepherd, he beckoned him into the princess's chamber, a warm smile etched upon his face. There, the shepherd's bravery and unwavering love were recognized and celebrated.

In the grand dining hall, where the wedding feast had been planned, the king greeted the shepherd, his voice resonating with gratitude. "Why did you shoot at my city?" the king inquired, his eyes searching for an explanation.

But the shepherd remained silent, his gaze fixed upon the deceitful captain and the princess, seated across from him. The princess's tears, borne from the depths of captivity, shimmered in her eyes, while the captain's unease betrayed his treachery.

Once the meal concluded, the princess invited her father to her private chambers. There, she mustered the strength to declare, "This noble shepherd rescued me from the clutches of bandits, where I languished within an iron cage. Even then, he wore these humble clothes."

The king, his heart swelling with gratitude and admiration, turned his attention to the shepherd. "And what shall be the fate of this deceitful captain?" he inquired; his voice laced with regal authority.

With unwavering resolve, the shepherd replied, "Let him meet the same fate he intended for me. Cast him adrift in a boat, devoid of oars or rudder, destined to wander the vast sea."

And so, the captain's treachery was met with fitting retribution, as he was condemned to the mercy of the open waters. The kingdom celebrated the shepherd's courage, and a grand wedding was arranged to unite him with the princess. Their union marked the culmination of a remarkable journey filled with valor and love.

As the wedding day approached, the kingdom buzzed with anticipation. The air crackled with excitement, and the joyous melodies of celebration filled every corner. The shepherd, now adorned in regal attire befitting his new station, stood at the side of his beloved princess, their hands entwined, their love radiating like a beacon of hope.

The ceremony took place in the grand hall of the palace, surrounded by nobles, courtiers, and the people whose hearts had been touched by the shepherd's tale of bravery. The king, brimming with pride and happiness, officiated the union, proclaiming the shepherd and the princess as husband and wife.

Amidst cheers and jubilation, the kingdom rejoiced in the union of their beloved princess with a man of humble origins but indomitable spirit. The festivities lasted for days, filled with feasting, music, and dancing. The king, grateful for the shepherd's valor and the happiness he had bestowed upon his daughter, bestowed upon the couple half of the kingdom as a testament to his appreciation.

Together, the shepherd and the princess ruled with wisdom and compassion, leading the kingdom towards a new era of prosperity and harmony. Their love story became a cherished legend, inspiring generations to believe in the power of courage, resilience, and the ability to triumph against all odds.

And so, the shepherd's tale, from a lowly guardian of sheep to the champion of love and savior of a princess, became woven into the tapestry of the kingdom's history. The legacy of their remarkable journey endured, reminding all who heard it that true strength lies not in wealth or status, but in the depth of one's character and the power of love.

And they lived happily ever after, their names forever etched in the annals of the kingdom, their story a beacon of hope and inspiration for all who yearned for a tale of true love and triumph over adversity.

About the Author

Karel Weinfurter was born on May 27, 1867, in Jičín, Czech Republic, to his parents, Karel Weinfurter and Antonie Jiránková. His father, a soldier in the Austro-Hungarian army, left the family soon after Karel's birth. In 1880, the family moved to Prague, where his father worked as a merchant.

During his school years, Weinfurter became interested in spiritualism after learning about it from his religion teacher. Along with his friends, he attempted to communicate with spirits and develop mediumistic abilities based on various instructions. It is said that he even received prophecies from the "spirit realm" before the death of Crown Prince Rudolf. Weinfurter's fascination with spiritualism consumed him to the extent that he had to leave school and was briefly admitted to a psychiatric institution.

In 1890, Weinfurter joined a spiritualist circle where he met Baron Adolf Franz Leonhard and Gustav Meyrink, who later became well-known writer. Together with a few others, they founded the Theosophical Lodge "U modré hvězdy" (The Blue Star), dedicated to the study of Theosophy, Freemasonry, Rosicrucian literature, and Indian philosophy. They also gained access to the writings of various mystics, although their understanding of these works was limited at the time.

They were initiated into society by Friedrich Eckstein, a prominent figure in European Theosophy and occultism. Through Eckstein, they were introduced to the German teacher of

Christian mysticism, Mailänder, whom they accepted as their spiritual guide. Mailänder's teachings were mainly based on the works of Christian mystic Jakob Böhme and partially on Rosicrucian symbolism.

Weinfurter's early employment included working as a postal clerk and an assistant to an art dealer. He also served as a secretary to the poet Jaroslav Vrchlický. During this time, he began his career as a journalist, writing reviews and articles for various publications. He also worked as an office clerk and an assistant teacher at Charles-Ferdinand University in Prague.

Later, Weinfurter became a translator and editor for the publisher J.R. Vilímek. Translation became his primary source of income for most of his life. It was during this period that his first book, "Divy a kouzla indických fakirů" (Miracles and Magic of Indian Fakirs), was published in May 1913 by Vilímek. The book went through three editions.

In addition to his literary pursuits, Weinfurter had various interests and hobbies. He wrote articles on sports shooting, studied music and painting, and developed a fascination with entomology, the study of insects. His expertise in entomology led to the publication of a specialized work on microscopy, which was used as a reference in universities. He even discovered a new species of fly, which was named after him.

After World War I, Weinfurter began collaborating closely with the publisher Jan Zmatlík. He translated and published numerous works of occult and spiritual literature for Zmatlík's "Knihovna šťastných lidí" (Library of Happy People). In mid-1921, he started editing the magazine "Okultní a spiritualistická revue" (Occult and Spiritualist Review) for Zmatlík, which was the first Czech magazine to explore the synthesis of esotericism from different religious and philosophical systems. It was in this magazine that Weinfurter first published an article on mysticism, describing mystical exercises. The article received unexpected attention, leading to several follow-ups.

During this time, Weinfurter faced criticism from Otakar Gries, a hermeticist from Přerov, who claimed exclusive rights to the correct (magical) interpretation of so-called letter exercises. Weinfurter defended his mystical interpretation (which he had learned from his Rosicrucian teacher) in the magazine, but Gries continued his attacks. As a result, Weinfurter decided to step down from editing the magazine.

Upon Zmatlík's request, Weinfurter began working on a more extensive work on mysticism. Little did he know that his life was about to take a significant turn. On Easter of 1923, his book "Ohnivý keř čili odhalená cesta mystická" (The Fiery Bush or the Unveiled Mystic Path) was published. The book quickly sold out and sparked a newfound interest in mysticism. Some Catholic priests even acknowledged Weinfurter's work. Monks from various orders practiced the exercises outlined in his book, and there was a growing interest in mysticism within the church, leading to translations of works by previously overlooked saints into Czech. With the support of a patron, Weinfurter started publishing the magazine "Psyche," dedicated to mysticism, in 1924. A circle of enthusiasts formed around him, which eventually became the foundation of the emerging organization called "Psyché." The society emphasized practicing the mystical exercises from "Ohnivý keř" and prohibited other practices. In addition to lectures, the society published various publications, including Weinfurter's own writings and translations.

In 1937, British journalist and researcher Paul Brunton visited Prague at the invitation of the society. Weinfur ter translated and published several of Brunton's essential books. Through Brunton, Czech mystics learned about the teachings of Mahārshi, an Indian sage whose teachings became crucial for the further development of Czech mysticism. Weinfurter was the first to translate Mahārshi's essential works into Czech in 1940.

The period of mystical development was abruptly interrupted by the onset of World War II. During the Heydrich regime, Weinfurter was arrested and detained. Shortly after his release, he fell ill due to the cold conditions in his prison cell. He passed away on March 14, 1942, in Prague.

Weinfurter's literary legacy includes over 80 titles. While many of these were pamphlets or abridged versions of more significant works, his most well-known book remains "Ohnivý keř čili odhalená cesta mystická." The book went through multiple editions and had a significant impact on the interest in mysticism in the Czech Republic. He also wrote an eleven-volume series called "Bible ve světle mystiky" (Bible in the Light of Mysticism), which provided interpretations and commentaries on selected books of the New Testament and several apocryphal texts from a mystical perspective. His other notable works include "Mystický slabikář" (Mystical Primer), a two-volume interpretation of mystical dreams, symbols, and secret characters of the Rosicrucians, and "Mistr Rámakrišna" (Master Rāmakrishna), a comprehensive contribution to understanding the life and teachings of the prominent Indian saint.

Weinfurter's translations were equally significant for the field of mysticism. He translated over 300 books, including works by Rāmakrishna, Eckhart, de Molinos, Blavatsky, Brunton, and many others. His translations played a vital role in introducing Czech readers to a wide range of spiritual and mystical literature.

Weinfurter's mysticism was rooted in both Western and Eastern traditions. He drew inspiration from Western mystics such as

Eckhart, Suso, Tauler, Ruysbroeck, and Kempis, as well as heretical figures like Böhme and the Quietists. From the Eastern traditions, he incorporated the teachings of Rāmakrishna and his disciples, emphasizing the original Indian Vedānta. Weinfurter saw mysticism as a means of bridging the gap between Eastern and Western religions, advocating for their synthesis. His mysticism did not reject religion but rather stripped it of dogma and served as an overarching framework in which Eastern and Western mystics could find common ground.

Weinfurter's mystical teachings were seen as an alternative for those who were unsatisfied or disillusioned with traditional religious institutions. His works and translations influenced many individuals in the Czech Republic who were engaged in alternative, non-denominational mysticism, such as František Drtikol, Květoslav Minařík, Jiří Scheufler, and numerous others.

Karel Weinfurter's contributions to mysticism and his exploration of esoteric traditions left a lasting impact on the spiritual landscape of the Czech Republic. His writings continue to inspire and guide spiritual seekers, offering a

synthesis of mystical wisdom from both the
East and the West.

Translator's Note

The fairy tales presented in this book, originally titled "O vílách a čarodějích" by Karel Weinfurter and published by Alois Hynek in Prague in 1920, showcase the timeless elements that define traditional fairy tales. These tales exhibit the classic motifs of a courageous protagonist overcoming obstacles, the inclusion of magical or supernatural elements, and the ultimate attainment of a happily ever after ending. The stories follow a familiar narrative structure and explore themes of bravery, love, and the triumph of good over evil. The characters within these tales are memorable, the settings are depicted vividly, and an aura of wonder and imagination permeates throughout.

In the process of translating these fairy tales, a conscious effort was made to infuse the passages with contemporary language and storytelling techniques, while still preserving the essence and integrity of the original tales. This modernization aimed to engage readers with a more relatable and accessible style, while staying true to the core elements that make fairy tales so beloved.

Fairy tales hold a special place in the realm of literature, not only for their entertainment value but also for their ability to convey moral lessons and ignite the imagination of readers. These timeless tales have been passed down through generations, enchanting audiences of all ages. It is my hope that this translation successfully captures the enduring magic and universal appeal of these fairy tales, allowing readers to embark on a captivating journey filled with wonder, wisdom, and the joy of storytelling.

About the Translator

Kytka Hilmarová, a Prague native and political refugee, embarked on a transformative journey at a young age when she and her parents sought asylum in the United States in 1968. As an accomplished author, translator, and publisher, Hilmarová has left an indelible mark on the literary world, bridging the gap between Czech literature and English-speaking readers.

With over 200 books brought to life as a prolific ghostwriter and a portfolio of translating more than 100 Czech literary works into English, Hilmarová acts as a vital bridge connecting Czech literature with a global audience. Her visionary approach and unwavering commitment to preserving and promoting Czech culture, history, tradition, and literature have ensured that the legacy of Czech literary works remains alive, vibrant, and cherished for generations to come.

As the founder of Czech Revival Publishing, Hilmarová showcases the rich tapestry of Czech literary gems, fostering cultural exchange and expanding the global reach of Czech authors. Through her captivating works and translations, she invites readers to immerse themselves in the enchanting world of Czech literature, offering a glimpse into its diverse themes, profound emotions, and timeless wisdom.

Join Kytka Hilmarová on a literary journey that illuminates the treasures of Czech literature, history, and tradition. Her exceptional talent, resilience, and relentless pursuit of bridging cultures make her an indispensable figure in bringing the richness of

Czech literature to English-speaking audiences, ensuring its enduring legacy for years to come.

10% of book proceeds support the preservation of Czech culture in the United States. Learn more about our efforts to safeguard and enhance Czech traditions, language, arts, and history through the following:

Czechs in America Organization (CIAO) is dedicated to fostering the appreciation, understanding, and teaching of Czech culture and history. We exist to preserve, promote, and support efforts to perpetuate the Czech culture, history, customs, and traditions in the United States. CzechAmerica.org

The Czech Museum was established with the purpose of preserving, collecting, exhibiting, researching, and interpreting a collection of artifacts and archival material related to Czech history and culture. TheCzechMuseum.org

Everything Czech is dedicated to fostering a profound understanding and appreciation of the unique and vibrant history, culture, and traditions of the Czech people. EverythingCzech.com